LET ALL
THE CHILDREN
COME TO ME

MaLesa Breeding
Dana Hood
Jerry Whitworth

Building the New Generation of Believers

COOK COMMUNICATIONS MINISTRIES
Colorado Springs, Colorado • Paris, Ontario
KINGSWAY COMMUNICATIONS LTD
Eastbourne, England

NexGen® is an imprint of
Cook Communications Ministries
Colorado Springs, CO 80918
Cook Communications, Paris, Ontario
Kingsway Communications, Eastbourne, England

LET ALL THE CHILDREN COME TO ME

Cover Design: BMB Design
Credits for Cover and Interior Photos: © Corbis, © SuperStock, © DigitalVision, © PhotoDisc, © Rubberball Productions, © Gené Photography, © Brad Armstrong Photography, © 2006 JupiterImages and its Licensors. All Rights Reserved.
Interior Design: John Baldoni
Interior Illustrations, except where noted: Aline L. Heiser

Except where noted, photos used are stock photos and not actual photos of children with disabilities, or of children mentioned in this book.

First Printing, 2006
Printed in Canada

1 2 3 4 5 6 7 8 9 10 Printing/Year 11 10 09 08 07 06

ISBN 10: 0-78144-404-7
ISBN 13: 978-0-7814-4404-0

Table of Contents

Foreword

This book grew out of conversations the three of us, MaLesa, Dana, and Jerry, had over the course of several months as we met occasionally for coffee and to share information about our lives, thoughts and views on a variety of topics. One topic that deeply interested all three of us was teaching children with disabilities the good news about Jesus.

It is a topic that is close to our hearts. MaLesa is a speech-language pathologist and Chair of Abilene Christian University's Department of Communication Disorders. She has worked in the public schools as a therapist with special needs students and is one of the founders and directors of King David's Kids, a Bible class program for children with developmental disabilities.

Dana is an early childhood specialist and Director of Early Childhood and Elementary Programs for Abilene Christian University's Department of Education. She teaches Bible classes to children of all ages, including many with disabilities. Dana is also the author of a Bible School curriculum and presents workshops around the country on brain-based learning and the development of spirituality in children.

Jerry is a special educator and Chair of Abilene Christian University's Department of Education. He teaches classes on methods for teaching children with special needs, and has developed and coordinated several grant projects on the inclusion of children with disabilities in general classroom settings.

Although we started out with the concept of writing a book about teaching children with disabilities in Bible classes we began to see our mission as much broader than that. Teaching, in a way, carries the connotation of something that is one direction: the simple act of dispensing knowledge. We teach, children learn. As Christian educators we believe that what takes place in the Bible class is, or should be, much greater than that. It is a place where faith is acquired and strengthened, where relationships are formed and deepened while God's grace and love is displayed, practiced, and shared. The Bible class is an experience, an opportunity, which benefits everyone who is blessed to be a part of it. The impact and power of that class extends far beyond the actual time we spend in a classroom.

We believe children who learn, look, act, and behave differently than the typical child should share just as fully in that opportunity. We hope that this book will be a resource and an inspiration to you as you attempt to help all of your students become a part of the Bible class experience.

MaLesa Breeding

Dana Hood

Jerry Whitworth

Dana

"What is the deal with this kid?" This was often the response of Bible class teachers who encountered David (not his real name) for the first time. This particular Wednesday night class experience had been especially difficult. All of the children from kindergarten through fifth grade—about 90 children—were in one special combined class that night. This was an overwhelming experience for David. He was over-stimulated and could not calm down.

By the end of the class time, his teacher was frustrated and angry. She could not imagine a child acting like David did. When she corrected him for his behavior he looked at her and told her she was mean. This was too much! Weren't children supposed to be respectful at church? "I told him that I would not accept that!" she told me.

"Well," I said. "The first thing you need to know is that I love this kid." Then I explained to her that David had several challenges out of his control, including Tourette's syndrome and ADHD. Despite these challenges, David is an amazing kid. He knows God's Word better than most of the children in the class. His talent in art is exceptional. Often, he is the first to ask that we recognize the special accomplishments of others. There is no child in that group of 90 children with a purer heart or a stronger desire to please God.

Despite all his gifts, David's behavior continued to frustrate his teachers who did not know how to respond to his unusual behavior. All they could see was problems—not promise. The only solution they can think of was to remove him from the class.

I went home that night and prayed for my little friend, David. As I thought about the response of this teacher and got past my own frustration over her negative reaction to him, I realized that she had not been equipped to respond to David's needs. Her anger and frustration were normal responses when faced with the behavior he exhibited that night. I came to realize that this teacher didn't need my judgment, and by God's grace I had not responded to her in a negative manner. She needed help.

The more I thought about that conversation, the more I realized that there are "Davids" in churches all over the world. They have Down syndrome, autism, dyslexia, and many other challenges. Teachers who volunteer in their church's Bible classes are rarely trained to address the special needs of these children. Like David's teacher, they need help.

That is when the dream for this book was born. I felt God was calling me to do something for these special children of His as well as the people who minister to them every week. This was a task I knew I could not accomplish on my own. Immediately I thought about my friends and colleagues, Jerry and MaLesa.

And so here we are: three professionals with different experiences and specializations, but with the same passion. We all have a heart for the child who doesn't fit in or just can't keep up. Praise God we serve a Savior with the same heart!

We pray that this book will help you see the children with challenges in your church with new eyes. Hopefully you will find both information and practical strategies to help you in your ministry to children. Finally, as you work with all the children that God has placed before you, may you never forget the value of what you do. You are welcoming the kingdom of God. What an awesome and humbling task!

MaLesa

As the Chair of the Department of Communication Disorders, I am responsible for providing students a variety of opportunities to work with different populations of people with communication disorders. When the mother of a child with autism asked me to help her start a support group for amilies of children with autism and other developmental disabilities, I saw a wonderful opportunity. My students would have the chance to work with clinical populations that aren't available to other students. This was a business decision—a clinical decision, perhaps—or so I thought. Looking back, the creation of King David's Kids was a great decision. My students have learned more about autism and other developmental disorders by working with this group of children than they could have ever learned from reading textbooks. But the clinical skills and knowledge my students have gained take a back seat in comparison to the spiritual lessons they have learned.

King David's Kids is a support ministry to families of children with developmental disabilities. While parents meet to provide support to one another, the students use Bible stories, songs, memory verses from Scripture, and prayers as vehicles for communication with the special needs children.

One of the first things I learned from working with this group is that parents of children with severe disabilities rarely go anywhere together—by themselves, as a couple, or together as a family. Children with autism, for instance, scream (often for hours) if their routine is disrupted in any way. Parents don't go out to dinner together, they dare not go to the mall together and they often do not go to church—simply because they can't find anyone who has the skills and willingness to spend more than a few minutes alone with their child. Twice a month the parents of King David's Kids meet as a group to deal with their issues and to have an hour and a half together while we work with their children. In this way, we accomplish two goals: to teach the love and messages of Jesus to special needs children and to provide respite to their parents.

I enjoy working with the children of King David's Kids for many reasons. I love seeing how "normal" these children really are. These special needs children are more similar to other children than they are different: they play with their food; they become upset if they believe they are treated unfairly; they love music; they desire and seek our attention—and like other children, will do whatever it takes to get it. I love seeing the spiritual transformation in my students as they work with the children of King David's Kids. My students are blessed because they get to see how their work and their faith are connected. As one student wrote to me in her reflection on the experience, "I am not just a speech-language pathologist—I am a minister."

And so it is that I have embarked upon this journey with a group of parents, a group of students, and a group of children. My contributions to this book are dedicated to all of them because it is in their eyes that I have seen the face of God.

Jerry

I heard the sudden slap of the screen door signaling my wife's return. Looking up from changing my shoes in preparation for mowing the lawn I asked, "How did it go with the doctor?" It was a casual question. Susie had taken our six-month-old son, Josh, in for what we had assumed was a routine physical. However, there was nothing routine about this physical. Susie slumped in the chair across from me, staring silently at nothing in particular. In a quiet voice, almost devoid of emotion, she said, "His diagnosis is moderate to severe cerebral palsy. The doctor predicts that he'll never be able to walk or talk."

Not comprehending, I replied, "Who? What are you talking about?"

"Josh," she answered. "He says Josh has CP."

Nothing I had ever experienced could have prepared me for those words. After all, neither of us had suspected that anything was wrong with Josh. We had noticed that he cried more than his older sister had at his age and his eyes looked a little strange the way they sometimes tended to roll to the corners. And Josh did have this peculiar habit of becoming rigid when he cried and arching his back, sometimes making it difficult to hold on to him. But, that didn't mean anything, did it? There were no problems during Susie's pregnancy. The delivery was normal. Neither of us had any history of disabilities in our families. We knew this happened to other people, but not to us. Surely this was a mistake—a simple misunderstanding that would soon be cleared up. Besides, he looked so beautiful and perfect, sleeping peacefully in his carrier. How could he have a disability?

Susie and I were about to embark on a journey that many have traveled before us and many will travel after us. It has been a journey with its own scenery and experiences—much different than what we had ever expected. As a special education teacher I had worked with and counseled many parents of children with disabilities. I had laughed with them and cried with them, hurt with them and rejoiced with them. I thought that I saw in their eyes what it meant to be a parent of a child with a disability. But, I soon learned that you can never really understand what that is like until you look through those eyes from the other side.

It has been a journey that we did not choose, but one that we have been blessed to travel. We started on it, like so many other parents, suspended somewhere between hope and despair. For the 20 years since, we have found our journey to be filled with much more hope than despair. Along the way we have encountered ignorance, inflexibility, frustration, impatience, and disappointment. But, we have also encountered new friendships, a continuing surprise at God's capacity for love and strength, and the joy that comes from small and unexpected victories. Most of all, we have come to understand the enormous potential God has placed within each and every one of His creations.

In this book, MaLesa, Dana, and I hope we can share with you what we have learned from our collective journeys, from the battles we've won, and those we've lost. We want to lend our voices to the chorus that sings the praises of a God who loves all His children and calls them to come to Jesus.

1

Salvation Belongs to Everyone

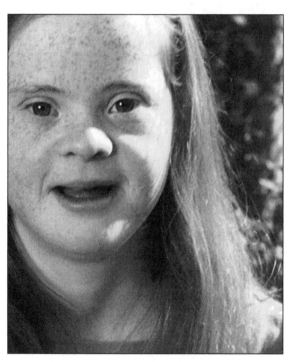

What is our responsibility to the child with a disability? These children don't always fit into the structure that we have created for those who can sit in a chair, listen without interrupting, and participate appropriately. I grew up thinking that God loved "these people" and that because of His love for them, they were saved. I still believe that to be true to the extent that it is true for you and me. We are saved by the grace and love of God. I recognize that salvation and the unfolding of God's plan for me has given my life extraordinary meaning. To believe that children with disabilities are simply saved by virtue of their disability robs these children of the richness that a relationship with Jesus brings. Furthermore, it gives us a great excuse to shirk our responsibility as a Christian to them. This chapter deals with the age-old confusion that we experience over salvation as it relates to people with disabilities and my personal journey that began with resisting the notion that children with severe disabilities could be taught about the concept of God.

A few days later, when Jesus again entered Capernaum, the people heard that he had come home. So many gathered that there was no room left, not even outside the door, and he preached the word to them. Some men came, bringing to him a paralytic, carried by four of them. Since they could not get him to Jesus because of the crowd, they made an opening in the roof above Jesus and, after digging through it, lowered the mat the paralyzed man was lying on. When Jesus saw their faith, he said to the paralytic, "Son, your sins are forgiven." **—Mark 2:1–5**

introduction

The Bible story on the previous page is heavy with meaning. When Jesus saw the paralyzed man, He didn't see his disability first. Instead Jesus saw in this man the same thing He sees in each of us. He saw a person for whom there was a plan of salvation. Jesus wanted this man to know that he was a child of God. His sins had been forgiven. Jesus looked into the man's heart, not at his body. Jesus made no judgment about the man's past. He didn't even ask the man about his sins. Jesus simply forgave the man. Salvation belongs to everyone.

We've spent a lot of time with that concept lately. If salvation belongs to everyone, then what is our responsibility to those people who learn differently? What would Jesus say? Would He say that because children learn differently or because they have behavior problems that they are exempt from His plan of salvation? How do we become more like Jesus? How do we look past the distorted body, the bizarre behaviors, the empty language, and look straight into a child's heart? Regardless of our expertise or experience working with people who have physical and mental disabilities, we all still struggle from time to time. But in those moments when we are compelled to look upon the heart of a child with a disability we'll see a person who is a child of God—not because he or she has a disability—but because that child is a human being.

This mother has lost her mind! That was the thought that flooded me as I sat in the board meeting. I had received a call from a mother of a child with autism a few weeks prior to that meeting. She invited me to attend the first board meeting of a newly-forming family support ministry called King David's Kids.

King David's Kids was in its infancy. I had agreed that my students and I would work with the special needs children while the parents met for support. Without the guarantee that a group of volunteers would keep these children, the parents' support group could not move forward. These volunteers couldn't be just any volunteers: They had to understand the nature of developmental disabilities; they had to be willing to work with the children in a large group; and they had to be willing to come back the following week.

My students are graduate students in communication disorders. They could gain a lot from the experience of working with children with developmental disabilities. Yet in this board meeting I was having second thoughts about my decision to volunteer my students and myself. The same mother who had asked me to join the board was now presiding over the meeting. She boldly presented the ministry's first mission statement: "To teach the love of Jesus Christ to children with special needs."

I had met these special needs children. Most of the children had autism. Some had Down syndrome. Others had rare disorders such as DeGeorge syndrome and Pierre Robin syndrome. Two of the children had severe cerebral palsy and were medically fragile. These children had serious issues.

Had this mother lost her mind? Did she know anything at all about children with autism? Perhaps I could get her to read some articles on "Theory of Mind." She needed to understand that children with autism can't take someone else's perspective. These children can't have relationships with other human beings. How were my students and I supposed to teach them to have a relationship with Jesus?

Resistance to change takes many forms. My form of resistance was to intellectualize this new notion that was presented to me—the concept that children with autism (and other disorders) could have a relationship with Jesus. To have a relationship with a man who lived and died 2,000 years ago requires a great deal of abstract thinking—belief in the Spirit and faith in the unseen. I could cite articles and texts—many of which support the idea that children with autism could not be taught the abstraction of a spiritual relationship. These children are literal thinkers. They can't deal with what they do not see and experience for themselves.

I decided to move forward with this project anyway. I decided that I didn't have much to lose. Even if the children didn't learn much about God, they would be loved and treated well while their parents met for support. Even if these children didn't learn much about God, my graduate students would have had the opportunity to work with a population of children they wouldn't have otherwise seen. The children and I embarked upon a journey that has become the mission of my heart.

Today, I watch as Jeffrey reads a portion of the story about Jonah. I smile when Maria requests her favorite song "He's Got the Whole World in His Hands." A few weeks ago Maria went around the room with a Ken doll (who is dressed up like Jesus) and to each child in the room she said, "Jesus loves Harold, Jesus loves Jeffrey, and Jesus loves Maria."

I believe God sent these children into my life and my students' lives. These children have become our teachers. They have taught us about how normal they are in spite of their odd behaviors. They have taught us about their sense of humor (and about ours as well). They are not only capable of learning about God, but they are deserving of it by virtue of their birth.

Thank You, God, for the children of King David's Kids. Their lives have been given purpose by You and they have been faithful to it. You sent me teachers in the form of children. I would have resisted all others. Amen.

The Experts Speak
The Special Needs Child and Spiritual Growth

Very little has been written about children with disabilities and their spiritual development. What has been written suggests that spirituality is not necessarily dependent upon intellect. Anna Giesenberg (2000) has suggested that spirituality may be an innate feature of the human condition.

All too often, we assume that a child must express his knowledge of our faith in order to have a spiritual relationship with God. Reciting the books of the Bible, reading Scripture, and memorizing songs are all examples of a child's cognition (what a child knows). For many of us, the expectation is that children will demonstrate a certain level of cognition before we accept that their relationship with God is possible. But what about the child who can't read? What about the child who can't attend to the Bible story or the child who doesn't speak or hear? Must these children demonstrate the same levels of cognition in order to have a relationship with God? Is it possible, in other words, for Angela to understand God's love if she hasn't memorized the books of the Bible? Yes. Does that mean that I shouldn't expect Angela to ever learn the books of the Bible? No. It is important to remember that Angela may not learn the books of the Bible at the same time other children her age learn them—and that she doesn't have to in order to grow in the love of the Lord.

A few months ago during our church service, we stood to recite the Lord's Prayer, as is the custom for our congregation. I am always moved by the Lord's Prayer, but this day I felt especially inspired as my own voice was overshadowed by a beautiful chorus of men's voices from behind me. I was so taken by the sound of these voices lifting up the words we were taught to pray over 2,000 years ago that I became silent just so I could hear them. As we ended the prayer and took our seats, I looked over my shoulder. What I saw brought tears to my eyes. In the row behind me sat five men, all of whom are known to have developmental disabilities and reside in an assisted living home. They were blessing me!

There is a beautiful lesson in this for all of us. Spiritual development is a life-long process. If Angela can't recite the books of the Bible today, take heart. It doesn't mean she will never learn them. Nor does it mean that she can't move forward in her spiritual growth.

Families of Special Needs Children and the Church

Belva Collins (2001) and her colleagues have written that families who have religious ties tend to have better coping skills in dealing with the added

"Families... need more than our prayers. They need to see us embrace their children."

stress that is often present when children have disabilities. Louise Jones (1997) is the mother of a child with a disability and the co-author of *Extraordinary Kids*. In this book she suggests that parents of disabled children are not likely to visit a church without an invitation or knowledge that a program exists for their kids. These families have endured too many disappointments to assume that anyone, even the church, will accept their children. Many have been hurt by someone in the church and are understandably skeptical. It isn't likely that, if they have been rejected by one church, they will try another one next Sunday.

The experts suggest that the religious community has a responsibility to children with disabilities and their families. Special needs children must be taught strategies that will enable them to apply their religious practice into their daily lives, even if they fail to understand abstract concepts. Families of these children need more than our prayers. They need to see us embrace their children as we welcome them into Bible class. They need to know that their children will be safe and happy while they are there. Finally, these families need to know that we believe their children are deserving of the joy and hope that faithfulness brings.

> **H**ow, then, can they call on the one they have not believed in? And how can they believe in the one of whom they have not heard? And how can they hear without someone preaching to them? —**Romans 10:14**

Voices from the Classroom

It is one thing to speak philosophically about how children belong in our Bible classes. It is another thing to actually do it. Casey, Angela, Harry, and Anna have taught me a lot about how to teach children with developmental disabilities. Let's examine each of their cases as voices from the classroom.

Casey Casey enters the hallway from the outer door. He is screaming with his hands held over his ears. This is Casey's usual entrance into King David's Kids. His adult buddy escorts Casey into a small room nearby. In this room Casey's buddy shows him a "social story" that says, "I will stop screaming. Now I am ready to play." The words have pictures above them so that Casey can interpret the written message as it is read to him. Casey immediately becomes calm, looks at his buddy, and places his hand on the doorknob indicating he is ready to enter into the playroom with the other children.

We still don't know why Casey screams as he enters our hallway. His language isn't developed well enough to tell us. His hands over his ears give us a clue however. The hallway is a narrow entry area. As Casey enters, the hallway is crowded with the parents of the other children who have stopped to greet each other.

Children with autism have great difficulty with a change in their routine. Many of them find extraneous noise extremely painful. The combination of these two things is enough to send Casey over the edge. We have learned to respond to Casey's needs by:

1. Not overreacting to Casey's behavior. Screaming is Casey's only way of telling us that he is upset, in pain, or both.

2. Providing Casey a quiet place for Casey to gain his composure. This allows Casey to get himself together and maintain his dignity.

3. Giving Casey a visual support system that reminds him of what he will do next. The written and oral message we provide to Casey helps him organize his thoughts so that he can focus on the evening's first event: playtime—a time that he enjoys very much.

Harry Harry requests a piece of pizza during snack time. The pizza is cut into small sections so that Harry and his classmates can have many opportunities to make verbal requests. Harry's buddy places a small cut piece of pizza onto his plate. Harry refuses the small square of pizza and says, "Pizza, please." Harry is encouraged to take the piece of pizza on his plate and then he will be given another piece of pizza. Harry continues, "Pizza, please." My students and I scramble to uncover the problem. We know Harry loves pizza. Maybe he doesn't like pepperoni. So the pepperoni pizza is replaced with a small square piece of cheese pizza. Harry responds with, "Pizza, please." Out of desperation I go to the kitchen to investigate the varieties of pizza. Surely there is a kind of pizza Harry likes. I see the pre-cut pizza slices in the boxes on the cabinet and it hits me. I grab a whole slice of pizza and carry it into the student working with Harry and say, "Try this." The student asks, "Harry, what do you want?" Harry says, "Pizza, please." A whole slice of pizza is placed on Harry's plate. He picks up the pizza in his hand and begins to eat.

Harry presents an interesting case. Harry has autism. This case is a classic example of autistic children. Harry loves pizza. Why wouldn't he accept our small pieces of pizza? A slice of pizza is shaped like a triangle. The pieces of pizza we were giving to Harry were shaped more like squares. It smelled like pizza. It had the same ingredients as pizza. But it didn't look like the shape of a slice of pizza. To Harry, this wasn't pizza. Interestingly, we have met several children since our first experience with Harry who will not eat pizza that is not in the shape of a triangle. Children with autism are very literal interpreters. Their thinking is rigid.

This rigid thinking can be seen in other examples as well. Maria loved the story of Jonah and the whale. We were certain that, because she enjoyed the story, she would also enjoy the activity that followed. She didn't. In fact she resisted participating in the activity by kicking and pushing away from it. After some investigation, we discovered the reason behind Maria's resistance. The Jonah in the storybook had red hair and wore a blue robe. The Jonah in the activity had blond hair and wore a green robe. An important modification for Maria is that the story characters must look the same. Now, Jonah looks the same in our activities as he does in the books.

Angela

As a new member of King David's Kids, Angela enjoys Bible story time. When the children enter the room for story time, each child sits on a colored spot in the circle. Angela sits in her special place too. She sits under a table—a place she has chosen for herself. Angela is not forced into the circle with the other children. Instead, she is allowed to sit under the table where she can see the book and hear the story. Her buddy sits with her. Soon Angela will join the other children in the circle.

> ❝ **Treating children "fairly" does not mean treating them "equally."** ❞

Angela sits under the table during story time. Consider these arguments against Angela's behavior. Shouldn't she be expected to do the same things the other children are expected to do? It isn't fair to have a different expectation for one child. Everyone has to be treated the same.

Richard Lavoie (1989) is an expert on children with learning disabilities and the author of *How Difficult Can this Be?* He raises an interesting point about treating all children fairly. Dr. Lavoie suggests that treating children "fairly" does not mean treating them "equally." Treating children fairly means giving each child what he or she needs.

In this case, Angela needs to feel secure. The small, darkened space underneath the table provides Angela with a feeling of security. She is the smallest and youngest of the children in the group. She is also the newest child to the group and doesn't yet fully understand the evening's routine. Within a few weeks Angela will join the group and participate in the same way that the other children do—especially if she is not forced to conform to what she does not yet understand.

But don't we want these children to learn something? Yes. We want them to learn that they are safe and that they can be happy in this place. Later, they can learn the content of what is being taught. There will be many opportunities for Angela to learn in the years ahead, what is being taught tonight.

Anna

Anna has difficulty sitting still for more than a few seconds in most situations. Her hands and feet are constantly in motion. As a result, she was previously allowed to roam the room aimlessly while the other children participated in story time. Now, Anna sits in her buddy's lap. Her buddy never forgets to wear her tennis shoes that tie. During story time, Anna unties her buddy's shoes and waits for them to be re-tied so that she can untie them again. Recently while playing this game, Anna's buddy didn't immediately re-tie the untied shoes. Anna spontaneously said the first meaningful word we have heard, "More!"

Anna may present one of the more serious concerns voiced by teachers. She is allowed to untie her buddy's shoestrings while the other children listen to a story. The concern here is that Anna isn't learning anything about the content of the lesson.

Anna is non-verbal and has severe attention deficits. Anna's mother reported to us that one of her first educational goals was to attend to a task for 10 seconds. The fact that Anna can sit for 10 minutes and engage in a shoe-untying task with her buddy is truly amazing. We are excited about Anna's progress, not because she is attending to the lesson, but because she is learning to attend to something—even if it is shoe untying. Learning to attend to an activity—any activity—is a necessary first step to attending to a lesson. I believe that some-day Anna will be able to attend to the lesson's content. Until that time, we will help her to attend to activities while exposing her to as much of the lesson as possible. Anna may not learn tonight that Noah built an ark, but she will learn, at the very least, that she is loved and included. Which lesson is more important for Anna to learn?

YOUR VOICE

Speak up, Speak Out

Our voice is an important element in this book. Whether you are considering ways that you might include a child with special needs into your classroom or you are simply concerned that your church may need to be more accessible to individuals with disabilities, your voice should be heard.

We should all be asking questions and raising our voices on behalf of those who cannot. Why aren't there more people with disabilities in our churches? Why aren't parents bringing their children to our Bible classes? Why isn't our church offering special programs to meet the needs of families of children with special needs?

Although serving a child with special needs may begin in the Sunday school teacher's class-room, ultimately, the ability to serve this child through his adulthood is dependent upon the entire church. What vision does the leadership of your church have for including people with disabil-ities? Have the leaders of your church issued a mission statement regarding individuals with dis-abilities? A well-grounded philosophy among the

> **We should all be raising our voices on behalf of those who cannot.**

leaders of any organization is fundamental to the success of such a program. We recommend that you use your voice to talk to your church leaders about a sense of community for everyone.

Use your voice to lead a discussion guided by the following questions: Are all members in the church treated fairly? Does everyone have an opportunity to contribute? Are individuals with disabilities really included in the worship service or are they relegated to a small section in the worship space? Are they greeted when they enter the church building or must they keep to themselves? Do we have enough accessible parking? Should we send teachers to seminars and workshops so that they can receive proper training? Because divorce rates among parents of children with disabilities is higher than average, what are we doing to minister to these families?

A church that is "inclusive" is grounded in an attitude of acceptance. Once this attitude is adopted it will drive the decisions and actions made by the church.

Lift Your Voice

Pray for God to open your mind and heart to all possibilities, for the children in your Bible classes and for yourself.

Pray for an inquisitive and curious mind about odd behaviors. Give God your automatic judgment of challenging behaviors and open your mind to alternative answers that God can place in your mind.

Are You Ready?

CHECKLIST FOR INCLUDING A CHILD WITH DISABILITIES IN BIBLE CLASS

- ◯ Evaluate safety issues and precautions
- ◯ Insure nearby bathroom facilities
- ◯ Have smooth flowing traffic patterns
- ◯ Provide a variety of textures and surfaces

- ◯ Have schedules appropriate to age level
- ◯ Alternate active and quiet time
- ◯ Where possible include indoor and outdoor activities
- ◯ Balance teacher-directed and child-directed activities

- ◯ Develop clear and predictable rules
- ◯ Have flexible schedule & provide regular routine
- ◯ Reduce distractions, both physical & verbal
- ◯ Build success into activities
- ◯ Use clear, positive feedback
- ◯ Use logical consequences
- ◯ Provide clear verbal and physical cues

- ◯ Organize all paperwork/materials
- ◯ Provide resources and areas to encourage good work habits
- ◯ Schedule both discussion and work times
- ◯ Locate and use all avenues for help
- ◯ Identify people with useful knowledge

- ◯ Engage the child's attention
- ◯ Prepare child for transitions
- ◯ Emphasize what needs attention
- ◯ Respond to and follow child's lead

- ◯ Visit and share information with parents
- ◯ Become aware of family/sibling situations
- ◯ Seek information from resource people
- ◯ Have a back-up plan

What I Think About Inclusive Bible Classes

Think about and write down your thoughts about the benefits and concerns of an inclusive Bible class for each group of people identified below. After finishing, discuss your thoughts with other members of your team.

	Benefits	Concerns
Children with special needs		
Other Children		
Bible class teachers		
Parents		
Church Community		

2

Think Inclusive, Not Exclusive

Moving Beyond Labels and Stereotypes

What's in a name?" Shakespeare asked. Well, plenty. Names and labels can be very destructive and harmful. They can limit our understanding and cloud our vision. In this chapter we will talk some about names and labels and how they have shaped, and continue to shape, our attitudes and perspectives toward disabilities. And we'll also discuss how those attitudes and perspectives, in turn, have shaped our relationships with people with disabilities over the years.

A *man with leprosy came to him and begged him on his knees, "If you are willing, you can make me clean." Filled with compassion, Jesus reached out his hand and touched the man. "I am willing," he said. "Be clean!" Immediately the leprosy left him and he was cured.* **—Mark 1:40–42**

What makes a really great teacher? Jesus has often been called "The Master Teacher." This title has usually been given to Him because of His unique gift of helping His listeners understand great truths in a way that was meaningful to them, for relating complex concepts so that everyone could grasp them, and for inspiring His listeners to take personal inventory and action in their lives. We often tell our education students to teach to "the higher order thinking skills." Jesus was certainly a master at that! His teaching caused His listeners to analyze, evaluate, and synthesize His message in ways that transformed them. These are characteristics of all good teachers. There have been other teachers who have excelled at these things. And, although He had these qualities in far greater quantity than others, Jesus' real gift as a teacher went much deeper than this.

We read in Mark 1:38 that Jesus was going throughout the countryside, teaching in the synagogues, and, as usual, great crowds pressed around him. They were anxious to learn from this teacher whose reputation had already spread throughout the land. Just as Jesus was finishing the lesson for that day, a leper appeared and fell down before him. Leprosy is a dreaded, ugly, and usually contagious disease that was somewhat common in Jesus' day. Those afflicted with the disease were separated from society and required to live isolated lives far removed from the rest of civilization. Often they were forced to reside in caves and special colonies where they were cut off from family, friends, and the rest of humanity. No one would get anywhere near someone with leprosy. It was a horrible, disgusting affliction. A leper was required to hold a cloth in front of his or her face, so as not to breathe in the direction of any one and to yell, "unclean, unclean!" if anyone approached as a way of warning them to stay away and keep their distance.

How would you like to live a life like that—so completely and totally alone? Have you ever experienced a time in your life when you felt completely alone? Totally cut off from the rest of humanity? Imagine what it would be like to have everyone you know run from you and shun you in fear and disgust—to be afraid to get anywhere near you, or even look at you. What would it be like not to know, ever again, the touch of another human being, to never feel another person's hand on yours? Such was the life of a leper—seven days a week, 365 days a year, year after year. That was the life of the leper who knelt before Jesus.

"If you are willing, you can make me clean," said the leper (v. 40). What an incredible statement! "You can heal me, if you will." Being willing to help, to reach out to another human being involves risk. We risk rejection, embarrassment, or perhaps even ridicule anytime we attempt to heal or help another person. How often do we have the power to help another human being, to ease a pain, soothe a sorrow, bring joy into a life of despair, to encourage, or lift up? Often we fail to make the effort. We have the power, but we are not willing to take the risk.

The leper knew Jesus had the power to heal him. Of that he was absolutely certain. What he didn't know was if Jesus was willing to take the risk. The leper was certain no one else was. We can almost hear the gasp and see Jesus' disciples and the others pulling back and covering their faces when they see the leper. How dare this leper intrude on them! He had no business being around normal people! They weren't about to have anything to do with him. He looked so awful—how could anyone bear to be near him? But, Jesus never budged or flinched as He looked at the leper kneeling before him. And then, in verse 41, we are told that Jesus did something quite remarkable, something incomprehensible, to those watching. It was what separated Jesus from the merely good teacher. We read, "Jesus reached out his hand and touched [him]."

" He touched him. "

Jesus touched the leper! How do you think that touch must have felt to the leper—to feel the touch of another human being—to feel the warmth of someone else's skin on his? Instead of the drawing back, hostility, and rejection that he was used to encountering, the man felt the acceptance and caring that he thought was gone forever. Jesus' touch, His emotional and spiritual healing, must have meant more to the leper than the physical healing that was to follow. In that touch the man's life was changed forever. And in that simple act, Jesus demonstrated what great teaching really is—He touched him. Without hesitation or fear, willingly and with compassion, Jesus did for this leper what no one else was willing to do. He reached out and touched him.

We encounter many children who need to be taught many skills: How to read and write; How to draw and color; How to recall information and take tests. A good teacher is adept at teaching all those things. Yet, there are many children who need more than that. They need someone who has the commitment, compassion, and courage to reach out and connect with them. They need someone to touch not only their minds, but to also touch their hearts and souls, to break down the walls and stereotypes, to look beyond the obvious, and see what lies beneath. And when we, as teachers, can do that we change our students, ourselves, and our world—forever.

While I was serving as superintendent of schools in a small, isolated school district in the Ozark Mountains, the Missouri Department of Mental Retardation built a small group home on the edge of town. The home housed eight to ten developmentally disabled adults in their late 20's and early 30's. All of the clients had cognitive disabilities, what would be called moderate mental retardation by most professionals. Although their measured I.Q.'s were in the 40-50 range, these men and women were much like anyone else. I visited the home on many occasions and found the clients to be friendly and industrious, despite the limitations imposed on them by their disability. One Sunday morning before Bible class, I made a reference to having just visited the group home. One young lady in the class, around 30 and otherwise fairly well educated, replied, "Isn't that where they keep those crazy people?"

Such has long been society's attitude of society about people with disabilities. It is an attitude of ignorance, misinformation, and mistrust. It is an attitude born of fear of the unknown, of those who are different in some way from ourselves, of those who do not behave or act the way we think they should. It is an attitude that has done great harm to people with disabilities and one which is still very persistent today, despite how enlightened we might view ourselves as a society.

People with disabilities have been with us since the beginning of time. Ancient writings refer to individuals who were imbeciles, idiots (probably references to people with mental retardation), deaf and dumb, and those with evil spirits (possibly people with mental illness or seizures). In general, people with disabilities have been treated very badly. Often they were executed, imprisoned, or used as entertainment for the nobility. At the very least, they were simply abandoned, ignored, and forgotten.

With the growth of Christianity there was some short-term improvement in the treatment of people with disabilities. This was a result of Christianity's emphasis on kindness, compassion, and service to the less fortunate. But, any improvement resulted from an attitude of pity and charity toward people with disabilities—not as an understanding of basic human rights.

There were also encouraging signs during this time. Reginald Scot, in 1584, wrote a book suggesting that some instances of demon possession and witchcraft were simply people with mental illness and that those individuals could be treated humanely. However, King James I of England considered the book blasphemous and ordered all copies confiscated and burned. The term "Mad as a Hatter" arose during this time as it was discovered that people who made hats, which were usually constructed of felt, often became brain-damaged from inhaling the mercury which was used to condition the felt.

In general, people with disabilities were viewed as being the cause of their problems. They almost always were distrusted, misunderstood, regarded as social outcasts, and sometimes even feared. They were usually relegated to second class citizenship, if they had any citizenship at all. People with disabilities were not allowed access to education, employment or other services, and were limited in where they lived, what they did with their lives, and with whom they could associate.

Negative stereotypes, discrimination, mistrust, ridicule, and pity are all attitudes that have defined society's behavior toward people with disabilities for many years. For much of modern history, individuals who were physically and cognitively challenged have had to face attitudes of discrimination, mistrust, misunderstanding, and even persecution. In media and popular culture, people who have disabling conditions are often portrayed as buffoons, evil, or in some

> **Most people are not even aware that they practice discrimination.**

way less than human and missing many characteristics possessed by the rest of society. It has only been in the last few decades that there has been any significant change in these attitudes and the treatment of individuals who have disabilities.

Unfortunately, a negative attitude and perspective toward people with disabilities persists even today. Much of this discrimination is much more indirect than in the past. Most people are not even aware that they practice discrimination in very subtle, yet harmful, ways. This discrimination is manifested in attitudes, language, values, and even our actions. These harmful attitudes are sometimes demonstrated under the guise of pity or charity—thinking that we are being helpful and kind. But pity can be very harmful because it can perpetuate an attitude and perspective that tends to devalue people with disabilities.

The right of self-determination—to make our own decisions, to live, work and play wherever we want, to form friendships and relationships, to establish our own goals, to realize our own unique potential, and to live life the way we want to live it of our own free choice—is a basic human right that all of us possess as a result of our humanity. This right comes from an understanding and acknowledgement that we are all created in the image of God. "Whether Jews or Greeks, slave or free—and we were all given the one Spirit to drink" (1 Cor. 12:13). We are all different and some of us may be more different than others. When we respect everyone and we treat everyone the way we want to be treated, then we don't create barriers that separate us from our fellow human beings. This is the attitude and example that Jesus gives us and that He illustrated in His interactions here on earth.

People with disabilities demand and deserve nothing less than we demand and expect for ourselves. So we provide access and services that not only allow, but also encourage, participation. We create a society where diversity is accepted, not out of charity, but out of recognition that we are all creations of God, loved and valued by Him. This recognition requires several responses from society. In our attitude and behavior toward people with disabilities we:

1. Think, see, and say, "People first."

2. Seek to include, not exclude.

3. Treat people with disabilities with basic dignity and humanity.

4. See all people as individuals with individual strengths and needs.

Society's behavior and treatment of people with disabilities has, historically, limited and segregated individuals with an enormous potential for enriching our culture and our society. Fortunately, this is changing, but there is a long way to go. We must adopt attitudes that see a person first without imposing assumptions and faulty beliefs systems on an individual just because we have chosen to label them. We must become more understanding and accepting of people who are different than we are, who look, talk, think, act, and learn differently than us. We must move beyond tolerating diversity and toward appreciating and celebrating diversity with a realization of what such an attitude can contribute to the quality of life for everyone. And, we must develop and implement policies and practices that seek to include everyone without excluding people based on some characteristic they happen to possess.

At one time, it was widely believed that people with disabilities were not capable of learning or even thinking. Society, in general, did not believe that individuals with physical or cognitive disabilities could hold a job, have families, or live on their own. Certainly they weren't capable of benefiting by going to church or Bible class. We now see these individuals doing all of these things and more. We have begun to understand that individuals with disabilities are limited only by our attitudes. Their abilities and potential have not changed over the years. It is our attitude and our understanding that has changed. Once we stop letting our attitudes and belief systems limit them, people with disabilities can soar and fulfill their potential—a potential based not on pity or charity, but on an understanding of the uniqueness and greatness that God has placed in each one of us.

When we do that we have begun to arrive at the same place Jesus was when He looked at the leper kneeling in front of Him and saw, not a label, stereotype, or someone to be feared and avoided, but a person in need of human understanding and acceptance. Jesus saw one of God's great creations.

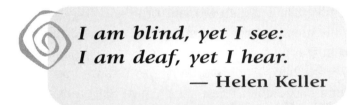

> *I am blind, yet I see:*
> *I am deaf, yet I hear.*
> — Helen Keller

▶ The Experts Speak

Noted author and proponent of inclusion, Shafik Asante, emphasizes the importance of language and its impact on our attitudes. The word "handicap" is a good example of this. "Handicap" has, to many people, a negative connotation. The word "handicap" originated long ago when people with disabilities were forced to beg on street corners. It has even been reported that some parents would purposely break their children's legs so that they would be disabled, generate pity, and get more and larger contributions. These individuals would hold out their caps to passers-by in the hope of receiving money. This "cap in the hand" practice came to be known as "handicap." This reflects a pervasive attitude that people with disabilities should be viewed as objects of pity—needing our charity, rather than as people entitled to the same opportunities for employment, education, and other "quality of life" rights as the rest of society.

This has often resulted in a form of discrimination known as "handicappism." An "ism" is what results when we believe that a label carries with it a set of characteristics. Once a label is placed on a person, that person also gets all of the characteristics that go with that label. The person becomes identified by his or her label. Whether or not all of those characteristics apply to the individual is immaterial. Society automatically assumes certain things about that individual because of the label he or she wears. Thus, we have sexism, ageism, racism, and handicappism.

> "When we can start seeing people with disabilities as people first... we can create the kind of community Christ had in mind."

As a result, rather than the disability being one feature of a person, it is viewed by society as defining everything about that person. The individual is confined and limited by the label. We assume certain things because of the label, and we place limitations and restrictions on a person as a result of that label.

This can be seen in the terminology used to refer to a person with a disability. We say "a blind man," or a "mentally retarded woman," or a "learning disabled boy." In other words, the disability is seen first and then the person. We allow the disability to shape our perceptions of whom and what that person is. We place restrictions and limits on him or her because of the disability. We may think, "Poor retarded Sally. Retarded people can't do this, so Sally can't do it." This attitude causes us to never really give Sally a chance to demonstrate what she can do.

In reality, all of us are different in one way or another. Most of us would resent having just one of our characteristics used to define everything about us. To define a person and limit him or her by one characteristic, even if that characteristic is a disability, is to shut that person off from society and to deny the potential that he or she might possess. Worse yet, it deprives the rest of us of knowing that person, forming a relationship with them, and benefiting from what he or she has to offer and to contribute to our community.

People with disabilities are more like everyone else than they are different. They have personalities and strengths, needs, and differences just like all of us. They are people with skills, abilities, personalities, and frailties, the same as anyone else in our society. That diversity is one of society's greatest strengths. It should be celebrated and appreciated. There are numerous examples of individuals with very debilitating disabilities who made enormous contributions to our society and to the quality of life on this planet: Helen Keller, Stephen

Hawkings, and Beethoven are obvious examples. We also find examples in the Bible of people with limitations, or disabilities, who were used by God for great and noble purposes: Moses was not a good speaker; Paul apparently had a visual problem; Zacchaeus was small in stature; Bartimaeus, though blind, exhibited great faith.

Our behavior is influenced by our values and our attitudes. Our language indicates our values and attitudes. When we can start seeing people with disabilities as people first, more like us than unlike us, and we stop letting labels dictate our beliefs and our actions, we can create the kind of community Christ had in mind when He said, "Let the little children come to me, and do not hinder them" (Luke 18:16).

Voices from the classroom

Labels

Stereotypes and labels can be used to separate and categorize. They can also hurt and limit people. The purpose of this activity is to think about how labels are used and can be misused.

Circle the labels that describe you:

boy	short	tall	fat
girl	skinny	happy	sad
athletic	honest	trustworthy	selfish
smart	blue-eyed	brown hair	blonde
funny	pretty	brown-eyed	plain
handsome	serious	intelligent	loves school
friendly	loner	hates school	social
easy-going	neat	musical	messy

Using the labels you circled above and any others you might want to add, write or draw a description of yourself.

1. Discuss with your class what labels are and how they are used. Explain how they can be used in good ways. Give some examples from the Bible regarding how labels are to describe people (Moses—the man of God; David—a man after God's own heart, etc.). Also, talk about how labels can be misused and hurt people. Have students brainstorm labels they have heard and perhaps been called themselves.

2. Use sheets with the following activity to help students discover how labels made them feel. (Prepare the sheets before class time. You will need one for each student.)

3. Use these questions to discuss what the students discovered about labels: How do you feel about the labels you chose? Do you feel that these labels give an accurate description of who you are and what your abilities are? What do you think are the advantages and disadvantages of labeling people and getting to know them only by how they have been labeled? What kind of effect does it have on people when you only talk about what they cannot do? How would you feel about someone else selecting the labels to apply to you?

Speak Up, Speak Out

Share your thoughts and reflections on this chapter by discussing the following questions with a friend or fellow teacher.

1. Have you ever been in a situation where everyone else seemed to be much better at something than you?

_____

_____

2. Have you ever been in a situation in which you felt different than everyone else or where you had a difficult time getting other people to understand you?

_____

_____

3. How did it make you feel?

_____

_____

4. Select two or three students that are particularly difficult to teach. Create a label for each that focuses on the child's positive characteristics and strengths.

Student	Student's strengths, positive attributes	Possible labels

Lift Your Voice

Lord, help me not to be blinded by my biases and perceptions. Teach me the harm that labels and preconceived judgments can cause.

Give me, God, an open and receptive mind to the possibilities and potential in all of Your creations. Give me the ability to treat others as I myself would like to be treated.

The words we use to talk about disabilities are constantly changing. Often words can convey the wrong image of being disabled. Being aware and sensitive is the first step toward correct usage. When you're in doubt, ask individuals with a disability for their preference. The key in talking about any disability is to place the person first so the person has more importance than the disability.

Vocabulary: Say It with Meaning

Say	Instead of
child with a disability	handicapped child
person with cerebral palsy	palsied, C.P. or spastic
person who has . . .	who is afflicted with, suffering from, a victim of
without speech, nonverbal	mute or dumb
developmentally delayed	slow, retarded
has an emotional disorder or mental illness	is crazy or insane
deaf or hard of hearing	deaf and dumb
uses a wheelchair	is confined to a wheelchair
person with retardation	retarded person
person with epilepsy	epileptic
person with Down syndrome	mongoloid
has a learning disability	is learning disabled
non-disabled	normal, healthy
has a physical disability	is crippled
congenital disability	birth defect
condition	disease (unless the disability is a disease)
has a seizure disorder	has fits
cleft palate	harelip
mobility impaired	lame
medically involved or chronically ill	sickly
person who is paralyzed	invalid or paralytic
person of short stature	dwarf or midget

From the book *Kids with Special Needs* by Veronica Getskow and Dee Konczal, reproduced with permission from Creative Teaching Press, Inc.

Labels in the Bible

Consider the Bible characters below:

Sarah	James	Esther
John	Dorcas	Timothy
Thomas	Moses	James

Look these individuals up in your Bible and write below the labels or descriptions that are used for them.

Sarah: _____   John: _____

Thomas: _____   James: _____

Dorcas: _____   Moses: _____

Esther: _____   James: _____

Timothy: _____

What do these labels tell us about these people?

_____

_____

_____

Think about these Bible characters: Samson, Bartimaeus, Paul, Zacchaeus. What are some of the labels used for these people?

_____

_____

_____

What are other labels we might use to describe them?

_____

_____

Attitude Check

The Bible teaches us that we should treat others as we would like to be treated ourselves. A first step in doing that is to determine how we feel and think about certain things and to try to put ourselves in the shoes of the other person. This activity is designed to help children without disabilities to reflect on their attitudes, beliefs, and behavior in regard to children with disabilities.

Check those which apply to you.

1. When I see a person in a wheelchair that appears to be mentally impaired as well, I feel
   - ◯ afraid.
   - ◯ embarrassed.
   - ◯ like crying.
   - ◯ like laughing.
   - ◯ like staring at them.
   - ◯ like talking to them.
   - ◯ like looking away.
   - ◯ sad.

2. People who have severe disabilities sometimes
   - ◯ are not capable of communicating.
   - ◯ don't notice other people.
   - ◯ are friendlier than other people.
   - ◯ would rather be left alone.

3. I feel uncomfortable around people with a disability, if I don't know them, because
   - ◯ I might say the wrong thing.
   - ◯ I might hurt their feelings.
   - ◯ I might injure them.
   - ◯ they look strange.
   - ◯ my friends will tease me.
   - ◯ they can't talk to me.
   - ◯ they wouldn't understand what I say.
   - ◯ I might catch a disease.
   - ◯ they act strange.
   - ◯ I'm embarrassed for them.

4. What I know about disability comes from
   - ◯ someone I know personally who has a disability.
   - ◯ television shows.
   - ◯ movies.
   - ◯ reading about them in books or newspapers.
   - ◯ things I've heard from other people.

5. When I think about disability
   - ◯ I wonder what it would like to be different from everyone else.
   - ◯ I think those people should be put in institutions for their own sake.
   - ◯ I hope it never happens to me.
   - ◯ it makes me feel scared, but I don't know why.

6. People who use wheelchairs usually
   - ◯ are mentally retarded.
   - ◯ can't work at jobs.
   - ◯ have people at home who help them.
   - ◯ don't have many friends.
   - ◯ are very nice.

7. When I see someone who has a disability, and looks and acts different, I think
    ○ he might be dangerous.
    ○ she will probably grab me if I go too close.
    ○ I'd like to talk to him, but I'd better not.
    ○ that person is just weird, and I don't want to deal with her.
    ○ maybe he needs help.
    ○ I wish I knew what to say to her.

8. I feel sorry for people who have disability because
    ○ they can't do all the things I can do.
    ○ they're probably unhappy because of the disability.
    ○ they don't get to do anything.
    ○ other people make fun of them.

9. When I'm around someone who has a disability, I feel embarrassed because
    ○ I can do a lot of things they can't.
    ○ they might be jealous that I don't have a disability.
    ○ it's not fair that they have a disability.
    ○ sometimes I make fun of people like that when they're not looking.
    ○ I don't know what to say to them.

10. When I hear someone making jokes about people who have a disability
    ○ if it's funny, I laugh.
    ○ I tell them to stop.
    ○ I don't say anything, but I feel bad about it.
    ○ I have some good jokes to share, too.
    ○ I think it's okay, because we're not telling it around the person with the disability.

11. The thing I'd like to know about disabilities is
    ○ how people come to have a disability.
    ○ what it's like to live like that.
    ○ how to talk to someone with a disability.
    ○ whether I should offer to help, or not.
    ○ how I might hurt people's feeling or insult them without knowing it.
    ○ if the person with the disability is angry with other people for their disability.
    ○ why some people have disabilities and others don't.
    ○ why kids with disabilities come to Bible class, even if they can't read or write.
    ○ how I can feel more comfortable when I meet someone with a disability.

3

What is Inclusion?

Hopefully the first two chapters of this book have called you to reflect on your attitudes and beliefs about people with disabilities. You have been challenged to look beyond the disability and see the person—a person with the potential for a rich, meaningful relationship with God. Still the questions may come, "So what? Why does this child need to be in my classroom? Couldn't she be taught better somewhere else?" In

this chapter we will discuss the benefits and challenges of including children with special needs in classrooms with their typically developing peers. In education circles this practice is called "inclusion."

When Mephibosheth son of Jonathan, the son of Saul, came to David, he bowed down to pay him honor. David said, "Mephibosheth!" "Your servant," he replied. "Don't be afraid," David said to him, "for I will surely show you kindness for the sake of your father Jonathan. I will restore to you all the land that belonged to your grandfather Saul, and you will always eat at my table."—**2 Samuel 9:6–7**

The life of David—shepherd boy and king—fascinates and challenges me. Walking through stories of his life we learn lessons about courage, worship, respect, struggle, repentance, and faithfulness.

One of my favorites is the story of Mephibosheth. (1 Sam. 20:14–15; 2 Sam. 4:4; 9:1–10) Perhaps this isn't a story with which you are familiar. It definitely doesn't rank in popularity with the stories like David's battle with Goliath. But it is a story that gives us a powerful picture of at least part of what made David "a man after God's own heart."

Before David became king, he had made a vow to care for Jonathan's family when he came to power in Israel. When the time came to fulfill this vow to his dear friend, David found that only one family member remained—Mephibosheth, Jonathan's son. He had been crippled in both feet at the age of five when he was dropped by his nurse while fleeing after the news of Saul's death.

David ordered that Mephibosheth be found. When Mephibosheth was brought before the king, no doubt he was frightened. He probably expected to be executed. He was, after all, the grandson of Saul, David's enemy. Added to this was the fact that he was just a cripple. How could he possibly be of any interest or use to this new king?

So Mephibosheth bowed before the king and awaited his fate. Then he heard David say, "Don't be afraid for I will surely show you kindness for the sake of your father Jonathan." This was incomprehensible! Couldn't David see that he was just a cripple? Mephibosheth asked, "What is your servant, that you should notice a dead dog like me?"

Do you hear the words, in 2 Samuel 9:8, Mephibosheth used to describe himself? It makes you wonder about the treatment he had received! Had his handicap caused him to be scorned and excluded? Well, that all was about to be changed!

David decreed that Mephibosheth be given the lands that belonged to Saul. He would be cared for and always have a home. But David doesn't stop there. He made the astonishing announcement that Mephibosheth would always eat at the king's table—no longer excluded, but now fully included.

Did David have to take this final step in order to fulfill his vow? Probably not. But his love for his friend and brother Jonathan was so great that simply providing for the needs of his son was not enough. His love compelled him to treat this disabled man with honor. He did indeed show Jonathan "unfailing kindness like that of the LORD" (1 Sam. 20:14).

If we are to be a people after God's own heart we can do no less than David. Love should compel us to show "unfailing kindness like that of the LORD" to those in our midst—including those with challenges. Consider what Paul charges the people of God to do in Galatians 6:2, 9–10.

*C*arry each other's burdens, and in this way you will fulfill the law of Christ.... Let us not become weary in doing good, for at the proper time we will reap a harvest if we do not give up. Therefore, as we have opportunity, let us do good to all people, especially to those who belong to the family of believers. —**Galatians 6:2, 9–10**

This passage is conspicuously lacking in qualifiers. It doesn't grant us an out if people are different, challenging, or disabled. This passage calls us to live the vow we make to one another when we chose to call Jesus our brother. If we want to be a people after God's own heart, then like David, there must be a place at the table for everyone—fully included, honored, and welcomed.

"Is there a place for her son in our church's children's program? She is really looking for a church and has been told more than once that, if she attends a church, she is expected to keep her child with her. There just isn't a place for him in the Bible classes." This was the question I was asked concerning a child with autism. What could I say? Didn't Jesus himself say, "Let the children come and do not hinder them"? (Luke 18:16)

The good news is that I could honestly tell my friend that our church's children's program is committed to including all children. We have worked with many children with various challenges—Tourette syndrome, Down syndrome, autism, cerebral palsy, ADHD, bipolar disorder, etc. When you ask the leaders of our children's ministry to name the greatest strengths of our program, our commitment to children with disabilities always tops the list.

This hasn't always been easy. There have been times that I, too, have left my Bible class feeling inept, inadequate, and ineffective. I have asked myself, "What in the world were you thinking when you said you could do this?" It is then that I have to prayerfully remember the commitment that God has called me to—a commitment to welcome all of his children.

When such a commitment is made, it must be more than just rhetoric. It will demand that we support, educate, and equip teachers. Sometimes this means recruiting a volunteer whose only responsibility in the Bible class is to help a child participate with his typically developing peers as fully as possible. Often it is frustrating and difficult. In the end it is always rewarding.

Did this parent's experience surprise you? Is it hard for you to imagine being told that your child isn't welcome in a faith community? The sad reality is that this occurs all too frequently. These parents, who are already facing more challenges than many of us can imagine, are told that the church has no place for them. They find themselves rejected and left without the spiritual support of God's people—disconnected from the Body of Christ.

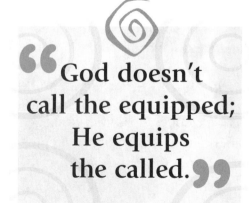

"God doesn't call the equipped; He equips the called."

So then, what do you do? Perhaps the idea of including these children in your programs still frightens you. You aren't sure you can really do it. That's okay. It only means that you are normal. But just remember that God did not give you a spirit of fear (see Rom. 8:15). In fact, reading this book is a great place to start! Just take it a step at a time and remember that God doesn't call the equipped; He equips the called. Is He calling you?

 # The Experts Speak

Inclusion is not really a new idea. In fact, the Russian theorist Lev Vygotsky wrote in 1925 that the thing most damaging to children with challenges is not the original disability. Instead, the most debilitating consequence is how the disability "changes the way the child participates in the activities of his or her culture." (Berk & Windsor, 1995, p. 83) These children, who already face more challenges than their typically developing peers, are denied access to the social interactions crucial for them to reach their full potential. Vygotsky stood as an advocate for including children with challenges with their typically developing peers, therefore providing them with better models and giving them the opportunity to participate as valued members of their communities.

This was a revolutionary idea. Remember, from Jerry's discussion in chapter two, that in the early part of the 20th century it was believed that these children could not learn. They belonged in institutions, separated from the rest of society. Vygotsky was definitely a man before his time.

More recently, the Individuals with Disabilities Education Act (IDEA), originally called The Education for All Handicapped Children Act of 1975, has established requirements for the placement options for children in public schools. The law requires that:

> to the maximum extent appropriate, children with disabilities . . . are educated with children who are not disabled, and that special classes, separate schooling, or other removal of children with disabilities from the regular environment occurs only when the nature or severity of the disability is such that education in regular classes with the use of supplementary aids and services cannot be attained satisfactorily. [IDEA Sec. 612 (5) (B)].

Philosophically, there is a movement toward a more inclusive society that does not separate and segregate individuals based on differences that are often misunderstood. Inclusion proponents argue that our schools must mirror this inclusive, diverse society (Gartner and Lipsky, 1987; Giangreco and Putnam, 1991). So inclusion is first an attitude—a value and belief system—not an action or set of actions.

Research indicates the relative failure of traditional pullout programs as a viable approach to teaching children with disabilities (Will, 1986; Affleck, Madge, Adams, and

Lowenbraum, 1988; Semmel, Gottlieb, and Robinson, 1979). The children in these settings often receive instruction that is less rich and often ineffective, while practices in many inclusive schools are demonstrating that teaching all students together in general education settings can be done successfully if appropriate practices and methods are used (Banerji and Daily, 1995; Bishop, 1995; Davis, 1995).

No one wants to be excluded. Inclusive education is about embracing all students—making a commitment to do whatever it takes to provide each student in the community, and each citizen in a democracy, an inalienable right to belong and not to be excluded. Inclusion assumes that living and learning together is a way that benefits everyone, not just children who are labeled as having a difference (e.g., gifted, non-English proficient, or disability).

> **"Inclusion assumes that living and learning together is a way that benefits everyone."**

Inclusion starts with an assumption that all students can do the same work and then adapting for those students who need it, rather than focusing on the "abnormal" or weaknesses and trying to "fix" the disability. The presumption is that the educational setting needs to change and adapt instead of trying to force the student to fit into an inflexible concept of "normal."

Is it easy? Truly worthwhile endeavors rarely are. However, it is an endeavor filled with great potential for the child with disabilities as well as for the typically developing child. Some of the fruits and promises of an inclusive approach include the following:

1. To provide an "inclusive" educational environment in which all children can succeed.

2. To enable children with disabilities to develop autonomy, independence, competence, confidence, and pride.

3. To provide all children with accurate, developmentally appropriate information about their own and others' disabilities and foster understanding that a person with a disability is different in one respect but similar in many others.

4. To enable all children to develop the ability to interact knowledgeably, comfortably, and fairly with people having various disabilities.

5. To teach children with disabilities how to handle and challenge name calling, stereotypic attitudes, and physical barriers.

6. To teach non-disabled children how to resist and challenge stereotyping, name calling, and physical barriers directed against people with disabilities (Derman-Sparks, 1989, p. 40).

This list demonstrates that inclusion can be a win-win situation. The benefits are not only for the child with disabilities. The typically developing children are also provided with wonderful opportunities for growth—opportunities to become welcoming and accepting individuals who look past the outside and see the person on the inside. That is a perspective that is consistent with the heart of God!

> **T**he LORD *does not look at the things man looks at. Man looks at the outward appearance, but the* LORD *looks at the heart.* **—1 Samuel 16:7**

Voices from the Classroom

Even the strongest advocates for inclusion admit that this approach is not without its challenges. It is an idea that is often met with resistance. What is the source of this resistance? Often it is fear. Sometimes teachers don't really understand the goals. Many teachers do not feel adequately prepared to teach children with disabilities.

Have you felt this resistance? That's okay. These concerns are valid. Your apprehension is normal. You are not alone. Let's explore some common concerns and misgivings about inclusion.

Common Concern #1

He can't keep up with the other kids. Shouldn't he be in a classroom where he can do the activities?

It is important to understand that this is not always the goal. Sometimes it is true that the child with challenges will not be able to keep up with the other kids. However, they often learn more than they would if they were placed in an environment separate from their typically developing peers. So sometimes it is appropriate to let go of the goal to have all children achieve the same levels of learning. This is true for your typically developing children as well. Every classroom, whether or not it includes children with disabilities, has a range of abilities present. Including children with challenges simply increases that range.

It is also important not to sell these children short. They will often surprise you. And even though they may not demonstrate their understandings in the same way or at the same time, they are capable of learning. Depending on the nature and level of their challenge, if they are given alternative ways to explore and express their understandings, many children can learn the same things as their typically developing peers.

It is important to remember that Sunday school programs are not only about academic success. They are places to build and practice community as the Body of Christ. So as you consider what to do with these children, remember that they have gifts to offer as well—insights and blessings of their own to share.

Common Concern #2

Why should I change things? The other kids like things the way they are.

This assumes that the children will not like any other structure or strategy that you might try. There are many ways to run a classroom, to teach a lesson, and structure a schedule. The other children will adapt to the changes that you make for their peers with disabilities. Soon, this new approach will feel just as comfortable as the old approach.

It is also important to understand that big differences can be made with small changes. Consider the following examples:

1. Allow children with attention or developmental challenges to hold a "fidget" toy during group time to help keep them physically occupied.

2. Use the "Clap and Remember" strategy in discussion times. After a child answers a question have all the children repeat the answer, clapping once for each word or syllable. This will help children stay engaged and give them a way to actively participate.

3. If you have children with physical challenges in your classroom use larger pieces of paper allowing them to use large movements associated with less mature developmental levels. Some children might do better if the paper is mounted to a wall or on an inclined surface while they work.

The strategies were adapted from an excellent book by Patti Gould and Joyce Sullivan, *The Inclusive Early Childhood Classroom: Easy Ways to Adapt Learning Centers for All Children.* This book is a wonderful resource full of easy to apply adaptations. While it is written with early childhood classrooms in mind, many of the strategies can apply with older children as well.

Another principle applies here as well. Often the strategies we employ to meet the needs of a child with a disability or challenge ends up being beneficial for all the children. Good teaching is often just good teaching no matter whom the audience. This will be discussed more in Chapter Four.

Common Concern #3   ## The other children will be afraid of her.

It is important to understand that the children will take their cues from you. If you are calm and relaxed the children will too. If you seem nervous or unsure, the children will follow.

In addition, it is helpful to educate the typically developing children. Like us, they are afraid of what they do not understand. One strategy for addressing this is to give children the opportunity to explore assistive devices often used by people with disabilities—Braille, wheelchairs, communication boards, walkers, etc.

One effective strategy is to incorporate sign language into memory work. In addition to helping build understanding for people with deafness, this helps students who are visual/kinesthetic learners as well as students with language processing disorders. Besides, sign language is fun and motivating for all the children in my class! Two wonderful resources to help you get started using sign language for memory work are the books *Sign & Say: Bible Verses for Children* and *More Sign & Say: Bible Verses for Children*, both available from Abingdon Press.

Educating children about people with disabilities in this way can provide powerful lessons even if there is no one in your church family who uses these particular supports. Through experiences like this you are preparing children ahead of time and giving them skills for life—life within the church family and the larger community.

When you teach about the healing miracles of Jesus, think about exploring various types of assistive equipment. The stories of the lame man let down through the roof, the man born deaf, and others provide wonderful opportunities to develop an inclusive spirit in children.

Children's books offer another avenue for fostering an attitude of understanding and acceptance. Many children's books describe and explain behaviors that individuals with disabilities exhibit. Other books help us see that these kids are children first! Don't miss the list of some outstanding titles at the end of this chapter.

Common Concern #4   ## I will be spending so much time with them that I won't be able to meet the other kids' needs.

The picture of Jesus the Good Shepherd is a powerful image. When we wonder if we should go to all this trouble for one child when we have so many others in our classrooms, we need to remember that we serve a Savior who left the 99 to find the one that was lost. No child is unworthy of our every effort to help him or her succeed.

Another important understanding, briefly mentioned above, is that many of the strategies we use to help children with challenges be successful end up being good for all children.

It just won't be fair when I do special things for him that I don't do for the other children.

This concern comes from a misunderstanding of what it means to be fair. Remember, fair does not mean doing the same thing for everyone, but doing what everyone needs. Here's a story to illustrate this: Imagine that you go to the doctor's office. Perhaps you are afraid that you have pneumonia. When you get into the treatment room the doctor says, "Well, let's get a cast put on that leg." You obviously protest saying that you do not have a broken leg.

The doctor replies that the first patient he saw on that day had a broken leg and required a cast. In his commitment to be "fair" to all his patients, he has to do the same thing for everyone. The point is clear. The children who come to us have a variety of needs, not all related to ability or disability. Any parent with more than one child will attest to the fact that kids need different things. So "fair" means that we will make every effort to adapt what we do to meet each individual child's needs.

Teachers often worry that the children will protest. There are not many of us who haven't heard a child whine, "But that's not fair!" Yet, children will nearly always understand if we take the time to explain it to them. "I am going to do my best to do what everyone in our class needs. Jonathon needs to play with the blocks during story so he can sit still. You need other things. I am going to give Jonathon what he needs, and I am going to give you what you need."

As we close this discussion about the benefits and challenges of inclusion, I (Dana) would like to share with you something I have learned to do in my classroom. There are times when the behaviors of children with disabilities can be frustrating for the other children. Particularly in the case of disabilities that include behavior challenges—ADHD, autism, etc.—I find it is my tendency to want to rescue the other children too quickly when they can learn something very powerful by practicing patience. Let me illustrate this with a story.

> "Living as the Body of Christ isn't always easy."

One Wednesday evening, Craig, a 5th grade boy with autism, was having a particularly difficult night. Like many children with this disability, when Craig tries to enter a social interaction, he is not aware of physical space and often gets right in another child's face. On this night, he was determined to interact with Robert. Craig was constantly sitting too close, talking too loud, and touching too much. While Robert was obviously not enjoying this interaction, he was handling it. He would gently, and repeatedly, tell Craig to move over. At other times Robert would just sigh, shrug, and let Craig stay where he was—much too close for comfort.

I would occasionally remind Craig to keep his hands to himself and use a quiet voice, but for the most part I did not intervene. However, when the evening was over, I pulled Robert aside and told him how proud I was of him. I reminded him that it is very difficult for Craig to make friends and he doesn't always know how to do it. I said, "Robert, I know this wasn't your most fun night in Bible class, but I really saw Jesus in you tonight. You were patient and kind to Craig. Those are fruits of the Spirit that I could tell God gave you tonight. Thank you so much for how you treated Craig."

In the best of situations, living as the Body of Christ isn't always easy. This evening gave Robert a chance to learn something about the love in 1 Corinthians 13 (RSV) that "bears all things." If I had pulled Craig out of class, Robert would not have had this opportunity and once again, Craig would have left feeling defeated and unwelcome. This is definitely not a feeling we want children to have at church.

Speak Up, Speak Out

YOUR VOICE

As you welcome children with disabilities into your program, the other children will make comments and ask questions about disabilities. This is particularly true for young children. They are curious about the equipment and devices people use for specific disabilities. Younger children sometimes even fear "catching" the disability. They need information, words, and support for handling these questions. Louise Derman-Sparks (1989) offers the following guidelines for dealing with these comments and questions.

For the child with the disability:

1. Find out how the child's parents are explaining the specific disability to the child and to others.

2. Help children find the words to answer questions for themselves.

3. Find out what the child wants you to tell other children.

4. Teach children that they have the right to choose to answer or not to answer another child's question and that they can call on the teacher to answer for them.

5. Show support for children's feelings about having to answer questions about their disabilities.

For the typically developing child:

1. Do not deny differences in the physical or mental abilities of people.

2. Do not criticize a child for noticing and asking questions about physical and developmental differences.

3. Listen carefully to questions to understand what children want to know and answer briefly. Do not belabor the response.

4. Do not lightly dismiss children's expressions of anxiety and fears about disabilities.

5. Use accurate terminology when talking with children about disabilities.

6. If you do not know the answer to a specific question, be honest about it. Tell the children you will try to find the answer during the week and you will get back to them.

Time to Practice

Read the following scenarios and write a response. Refer to the guidelines listed above. It is also important to gently, but very clearly communicate that it is not okay to exclude some-one just because he or she is different. You may want to ask a fellow teacher to try this with you. Come up with responses that would be appropriate for children of different ages, per-haps a five-year-old and a ten-year-old.

1. Regarding a child with mental retardation—"He talks like a baby! He needs to go to the baby class."

2. About a child with metal leg braces—"I don't want to sit by her. She's a robot."

3. Regarding a child with cerebral palsy—"He doesn't talk right. I think his tongue is too big."

Lift Your Voice

The Bible tells us that we have not been given a "spirit of fear." Pray that the Lord will remove your fear of working with children with challenges.

Pray to see the children in your classroom through the eyes of Jesus—all children, no matter the challenge.

People learn in different ways. Not everyone learns exactly the way you learn. Jesus used many different ways to teach people because He understood that people have different ways they learn best. How do you learn best?

HOW DO YOU LEARN?

What You Do

Use the following letters to agree or disagree with the statements below. Write the letters in the blanks provided.   **Y** = Yes   **N** = No   **S** = Sometimes

○ When the teacher is talking, I blurt out answers.
○ I have trouble waiting for my turn.
○ I love to talk and do it even when I'm supposed to be quiet.
○ I like to take a chance when riding my bike.
○ I like to play very quietly, usually by myself.
○ I enjoy jumping from task to task without completing the first one.
○ Following oral directions is always easy for me to do.
○ I always stay in my assigned seat.
○ Outside noises capture my interest; I can tell you what is happening.
○ I never interrupt my teacher or classmates.
○ I can always find my book or pencil when I need it.
○ I find that I cannot keep my mind on what the teacher is saying.
○ I need to move my body all the time, fidgeting or squirming in my seat.
○ I enjoy listening to the teacher—I can do this for a long time.
○ I can remember all the jobs the teacher or an adult gives me at one time.
○ I notice that I can be happy one minute and very sad the next minute.
○ I am unhappy when there is a change in the daily schedule.
○ I drop my pencil, papers, or books often. I can't help it.
○ I have difficulty making up my mind.
○ I am always one of the last students to finish my worksheets.
○ In my mind, I skip or hop very well. When I try it with my body, I can't do it.
○ I wish I could do better on tests.
○ I wish I had more friends.
○ I get upset with myself because I get angry often and easily.

Underline the things you said yes to. Then ask your teacher for positive ideas about your behavior in class. Ask your teacher to describe the ways your learn best. List them below.

From the book *Kids with Special Needs* by Veronica Getskow and Dee Konczal, reproduced with permission from Creative Teaching Press, Inc.

Let All the Children Come to Me

We all have feelings. We are sensitive about the way we look and what we can or cannot do. It can hurt if others point out or make fun of the way we look or the way we do things. In the Bible, there are many examples of people who looked different. Zaccheus was very short and had to climb a tree to see over the crowd. A group of boys teased Elisha because he had no hair. What are you sensitive about?

FEELINGS

We all have feelings, too. We are sensitive about the way we look and what we can or cannot do. We are sensitive about what other people may think or say about us. It can hurt if other people point out, or make fun of, the way we look or the way we do things.

- ◯ my glasses
- ◯ my athletic ability
- ◯ my grades
- ◯ my blindness
- ◯ my hair
- ◯ my bowed legs
- ◯ my hands
- ◯ my braces
- ◯ my hearing aid
- ◯ my scars
- ◯ my height
- ◯ my cane

- ◯ my shape
- ◯ my feet
- ◯ my toes
- ◯ my fingernails
- ◯ my voice
- ◯ my freckles
- ◯ my clothes
- ◯ my laugh
- ◯ my complexion
- ◯ my moles
- ◯ my coordination
- ◯ my musical ability

- ◯ my crooked spine
- ◯ my nearsighted vision
- ◯ my crossed eyes
- ◯ my nose
- ◯ my crutches
- ◯ my writing
- ◯ my deafness
- ◯ my shape
- ◯ my dimples
- ◯ my speech
- ◯ my ears
- ◯ my teeth

From the book *Kids with Special Needs* by Veronica Getskow and Dee Konczal, reproduced with permission from Creative Teaching Press, Inc.

What do you think when other people stare or make comments about any of the items you checked above? How does it make you feel? Why do you think people do that? How do you think we should think, act, and talk when we see someone who looks or acts or does things differently than other people?

BOOKS

Most of these books are from secular publishers but lend themselves beautifully to Christian application. These are just a few of the books that are available. There are many more wonderful titles out there. Spend some time exploring at your favorite bookstore or website. Ask a local school librarian. Have fun discovering new ways to teach your kids to love all of God's children!

Mama Zooms! by Jane Cowen-Fletcher (PreK–1st) This is the story of a child who loves to sit on his mother's lap, riding in her wheelchair.

Howie Helps Himself by Joan Fassler (PreK–2nd) Howie, a child with cerebral palsy, wants more than anything else to be able to move his wheelchair by himself.

Friends at School by Rochelle Burnett (PreK–2nd) Using photos of many children with different abilities and challenges, this book illustrates the true meaning of the word inclusion.

Susan Laughs by Jeanne Willis (PreK–2nd) With simple rhyming text and soft pencil-and-crayon illustrations, the reader is introduced to a spirited little redheaded girl named Susan.
It is not until the last page that the reader discovers that Susan uses a wheelchair.

My Friend Isabelle by Eliza Woloson (PreK–2nd) A little boy named Charlie introduces us to his friend Isabelle, a little girl with Down syndrome. But this doesn't matter to Charlie. "Mommy says," Charlie explains, "that differences are what make the world so great."

Robert and His Yellow Frisbee by Mary Thompson (1st–5th) This is the story of a little boy named Robert who has autism, his sister Rosie, and a new girl at school named Sarah. Sarah sees Robert and is curious. Rose helps her and the reader understand her brother. At the end of this book Thompson provides factual information about autism.

Ian's Walk by Laurie Lears (1st–5th) A little girl named Julie tells about an outing with her brother Ian who has autism. This book helps the reader understand the feelings of siblings of children with this disorder. It doesn't provide a great deal of specific information, but still provides a springboard for discussion and understanding.

Be Good to Eddie Lee by Virginia Fleming (1st–5th) Christy, who has been told by her mother to be "good to Eddie Lee," her neighbor with Down syndrome, at first excludes him when she sets off with another friend. In the end Christy comes to appreciate her friend Eddie Lee in a new way.

Zoom! By Robert Munsch (K–3rd) This hilarious story about strong-willed Laretta who insists on buying the most powerful wheelchair available gives a positive message about young people with disabilities. Without making an issue of her challenges the author presents a character all children can identify with.

Now One Foot, Now the Other by Tomie dePaola (K–3rd) When his grandfather suffers a stroke, Bobby teaches him to walk, just as his grandfather had once taught him.

I Have a Sister, My Sister Is Deaf by Jeanne Whitehouse Peterson (K–5th) A young deaf child who loves to run and jump and play is affectionately described by her older sister.

We Can Do It! By Laura Dwight (PreK–2nd) Beautiful, sensitive photographs show five pre-school children, each with some type of disability. Nonetheless, they all lead full, happy, and productive lives because they believe, "We can do it!"

4

Teaching Children with Disabilities

They are called by many names and many labels: at-risk, slow learner, under achiever, special needs. They are the students who don't quite fit in with the rest of the class, who sit in the back of the room and never participate, never volunteer. These are the students who are frequently absent, who never complete class assignments, who never seem to know what's going on. But, they are the students you look for whenever there's a problem or a disturbance. These are the students that we don't know what to do with. Sometimes we secretly wish those students would just go away. These children find it a challenge to learn and we find them a challenge to teach. Yet, they are the students who need us most of all.

In this chapter we will talk about a group of children we have all had in our Bible classes. They do not have obvious disabilities. They look like all the other children, and yet there is something distinctly different about them. These students have problems learning, behaving appropriately, and in getting along with peers and adults. Who are these children and how do we reach them?

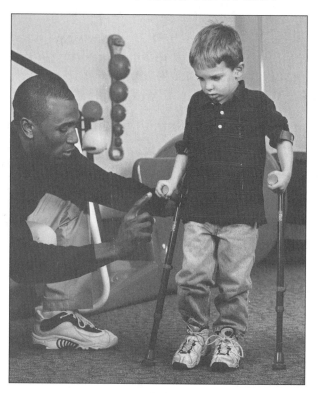

*Jesus went up on a mountainside and called to him those he wanted, and they came to him. He appointed twelve—designating them apostles—that they might be with him and that he might send them out to preach and to have authority to drive out demons. These are the twelve he appointed: Simon (to whom he gave the name Peter); James son of Zebedee and his brother John (to them he gave the name Boanerges, which means Sons of Thunder); Andrew, Philip, Bartholomew, Matthew, Thomas, James son of Alphaeus, Thaddaeus, Simon the Zealot and Judas Iscariot, who betrayed him. —**Mark 3:13–19**

Twelve men: a diverse lot, not very impressive. They were poor, uneducated, settled farmers, fishermen, and even one tax collector, (one of the most detested groups in society). They had many weaknesses and foibles. Yet, these were the men whom Jesus selected to be His closest companions, to carry His work and message to the world. Who would have thought that this group of bedraggled, unkempt outcasts could be successful? Yet, Jesus was incisive at discovering hidden talents and inner strengths and adept at looking through what society might view as problems and shortcomings while seeing people's untapped potential. He was able to mold these men into what He knew they could become. That unleashed potential would soon spread the Gospel across continents and throughout the known world. Within a few short years, when Jesus' followers came into a far off corner of the empire, it was reported that, "These men who have caused trouble all over the world have now come here" (Acts 17:6). Within a few short decades even the proud Roman Emperor would bow his knee to the teachings of this simple Galilean carpenter.

How could men like the impulsive, hyperactive Peter, James, and John with their quick, difficult-to-control tempers, or Thomas, full of doubts, accomplish this? If we had encountered these individuals in a typical classroom, many of us would never have believed they were capable of learning or achieving very much. We might spend considerable time trying to label and categorize them—to figure out why it would be difficult to teach them.

But, Jesus didn't waste time trying to label His apostles, put them in boxes, or focus on the things they couldn't do. He saw them not as they were, but as they could be. Jesus treated each man as an individual, giving just the right teaching, experience, and guidance that each of them needed. We, as teachers, can learn much from Jesus' ability to see strengths instead of weaknesses. From Jesus' example we can learn to focus on what children can do rather instead of what they can't. As a result, we tap our students' undiscovered talents and abilities.

The Problem with Labels

"What do we call him?" For countless hours I have sat in meetings with school staff looking at extensive evaluation reports on a student, trying to figure out what to do. Many of our discussions center around what label to pin on the student. We know he or she is having problems in school. We have completed many tests and now the main issue is, "What do we call him or her?" In the public schools, a student needs a label to get special help. Whether the label is learning disabled, mentally retarded, autistic, whatever, that label is necessary before services can be provided. We must have a name or a reason for why a student is having trouble behaving or learning.

This is unfortunate because there are a number of problems with labeling. They create stereotypes that cause us to affix certain characteristics or make assumptions about the child simply because of a label. An enormous amount of time, energy, and money is often poured into trying to determine the appropriate label when actually most of the data we collect tells us very little about how to teach the child. Labeling also tends to segregate children because we use the labels to categorize and separate. Perhaps the greatest problem with labeling, though, is that it can lead to rationalization. Often, once a label is applied to a child, we use that label as a rationale for not trying to teach the child. We say, "Oh, he's ADHD, so I can't do anything with him," or "She's autistic. I don't know anything about autism, so I can't help her." In other words, we tend to focus on the label rather than on what the child needs.

That's not to say that there aren't some practical and useful reasons why we do label. Labels help to focus attention on a particular type of disability, making it possible to receive needed resources. Labels also allow professionals and others to communicate and share research, approaches, and information. They also make it easier to group and organize characteristics and teaching strategies.

> **We... can learn much from Jesus' ability to see strengths instead of weaknesses.**

In the next chapter MaLesa will talk about specific categories of disabilities, their characteristics and what those characteristics tell us about effective instructional approaches.

In this chapter, though, we will talk about disabilities in a more general context: in terms of similarities in characteristics and learning needs. This is particularly important to do in terms of what are called mild disabilities. These include a broad range of disability types such as learning disabilities, mental retardation (in the mild ranges), attention deficit disorders, behavior/emotional disorders, and some forms of pervasive developmental disabilities.

Children with these mild disabilities have many things in common. Such mild disabilities are sometimes called high incidence disabilities because they are more prevalent. You are likely to have a number of children with one of these disabilities in your classroom. Mild disabilities are more difficult to diagnose because these children look and act much the same as any other children. As a result, they often are not diagnosed early in their lives. Their problems often do not become apparent, or at least do not cause difficulty, until they are seen with a large number of other children and are expected to participate in certain learning, social, or behavioral activities.

Another difficulty in teaching students with mild disabilities is differentiation in diagnosis. It is sometimes hard to tell the difference between students who have a mild disability and those who have learning, behavioral, or social problems due to other reasons such as environment, family background, personal history, poor teaching, lack of adequate role models, etc. Both groups of students are below grade level in reading and other academic areas, have poor social skills, have difficulty attending to and completing tasks, and other problems. That is why it is sometimes counterproductive to spend much time and resources in trying to label these children. Many times we don't know the reason, or reasons, why a child has trouble learning, behaving appropriately, or forming meaningful social relationships. Instead, we should focus our attention on ways to reach these children, helping them learn, developing effective social skills, and participating successfully in their communities.

Our role as Bible class teachers is to find ways to help these children learn about God's Word, to apply that Word to their lives, and to become faithful children and servants of our Lord. We will be more successful in accomplishing this if we focus on the child's strengths and see each one as unique and capable of learning and being blessed by being in our class and, in turn, blessing us. The learning needs of all students can be better served by not concentrating so much on labels and deficits as on specific strategies to help each child benefit from being in a Bible class.

As a Bible class teacher you have a unique and wonderful opportunity to reach these children, to touch their lives and help them find and use their special gifts. The poem, *The Key Makers* says,

Some people see a closed door and they turn the doorknob.
If the door doesn't open, they turn away.

Others see a closed door, and turn the doorknob.
If the door doesn't open, they try a key.

If the key doesn't fit, they turn away.
A rare few see a closed door and turn the doorknob.

If the door doesn't open, they try a key.
If the key doesn't fit, they make one.

(Author Unknown)

Some students learn easily and with very little teaching effort on our part. For others, we have to dip into our bag of tricks and use all the ideas and strategies we've been taught. For some students, though, none of the keys, the ideas, or the techniques we've been given work. With these students we must be creative, committed, persistent, and passionate enough to make the key—the ideas, approaches, techniques, or whatever they need to open their minds and hearts to allow them to understand God's Word and His Will. That will allow these students to become the people He created them to be.

The Experts Speak

Although much has been written on the subject, no one really knows why some children have so much difficulty learning and why they present such a challenge to those of us who teach. The number of children who are at-risk in our schools is a growing concern to many in our nation (Austin and Meister, 1990; McPartland and Slavin, 1990). Some have put the number as high as one-third of the school-age population (Roeser, Eccles, and Sameroff, 2000). There are vast cultural and social forces creating circumstances which place more and more students at-risk of failure, from school and from life (Barr and Parrett, 1995, Johnson, 1998; Mercer and Mercer, 2001). Smith, Polloway, Patton, and Dowdy (1998) define these students as "at-risk for developing achievement and behavior problems that could limit their success in school and as young adults."

Though it is difficult, and somewhat dangerous, to make generalizations, there are certain characteristics, identified in the literature, that do tend to be present in many students with mild disabilities as well as most children who have trouble with learning, behavior, and social tasks for whatever reason. General characteristics of these children include:

Educational

- Lack of interest in schoolwork
- Inadequate long-term memory
- Prefer concrete rather than abstract lessons
- Weak listening skills
- Low achievement in academic subjects, especially reading
- Limited verbal and/or writing skills
- Right hemisphere preference in learning activities (They respond better to concrete, sequential activities.)
- Respond better to active rather than passive learning tasks
- Have areas of talent or ability that are overlooked in school
- Prefer to receive special help in the regular classroom rather than in a special class
- Have higher dropout rates than other students
- Achieve in accordance with teacher expectations (Teachers do not expect them to be good students and accomplish much. Students perform to those expectations.)
- Require modifications in classroom instruction
- Distractable (They have difficulty staying focused and on task.)
- Poor executive control (They have difficulty monitoring and self-regulating their behavior and learning.)

- Poor strategic learners (They are not proficient at developing, implementing, and evaluating the success of a plan to accomplish a behavioral, social, or learning task.)

Social/Behavioral

- External locus of control (They tend to believe that they have no control over what happens to them. Everything is the result of luck or fate, the way they were born, whether or not the teacher likes them, etc. As a result, they do not believe that there is any connection between the amount of effort they put into a task and their success with that task.)

- Learned helplessness (They have learned not to try and so act helpless because they have found that people will not expect them to do things if they act like they're not capable of doing them.)

- Negative attributes (They see themselves in a very negative light—as being poor students, not smart, not capable.)

- Frustration (If they are constantly required to do things they are not successful at doing, they get frustrated.)

- Poor social skills

- Discipline problems (Behavior problems arise as the result of other factors, avoidance of undesirable tasks or of being embarrassed, attention-seeking, frustration, etc.)

Such characteristics can have a number of consequences for the child—many of them long-term. These might include:

- Negative attitude toward traditional learning environments

- Drop out of school, of Bible class, or church activities

- Lack of motivation

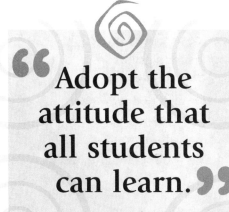
Adopt the attitude that all students can learn.

- Behavior problems

- Poor employment prospects

- Poor relationships with peers and adults

- Social adjustment problems

The above characteristics can create tremendous barriers to a child in traditional learning situations and as well cause great challenges for the child, the teacher, and the other children. However, as we discuss in the next section, there are some things you, as the Bible class teacher, can do to help these children and assist them in being successful students of God's Word.

Voices from the Classroom

Children of Challenge

Regardless of the causes, there are some specific actions that we can take to help children of challenge succeed in learning and in life. There have been a number of practices and approaches identified in the literature that hold promise for these children. These can help the Bible class teacher in effectively meeting the challenges such children present. In later chapters we will talk about specific teaching strategies that you will find useful. There are some general approaches to teaching and reaching children of challenge. The following are ten practices that, if incorporated into your class, can transform frustrated learners into successful learners.

1. **Adopt the attitude that all students can learn.**

   Attitude is a powerful force. It is the first step in successfully helping challenging students. If we have the attitude that all children can learn, we will translate that attitude into action. We will demonstrate tenacity about learning God's Word and an understanding of how that Word can transform our lives and the lives of our students. It may be easier, and certainly more convenient, to just let go and allow some children to drift away. We must persist until all of our students are learning. More importantly, we must communicate our attitude to our students. They need to understand from our words and actions that we will not give up on them.

2. **Pay attention to them.**

   As teachers we tend to ignore children of challenge. But they have been ignored all of their lives. Make an effort to notice them, make positive comments to them, and smile at them. Call on these students more often, but do it in a way that will enable them to experience success. Seek ways to include them, but don't do it gratuitously or in a condescending manner. They have encountered that type of attitude far too often. If we make the effort to act genuinely interested in these students, we will eventually see them respond. One useful way to do this is to choose one child in particular. Decide, for a period of time, to make an effort to pay attention to that child, spend time with him or her as a friend, and a role model. You may be surprised at the positive difference you will see.

3. **Help them to see the connection between effort and success.**

   Children who are challenged learners often feel that they have no control

Let All the Children Come to Me

54

over what happens to them and over the consequences of their life. They view the control for their life residing in external circumstances and forces, such as luck. As a result, they feel that it is useless for them to try to succeed in learning or in life, since their efforts have nothing to do with their success. Bible class teachers can empower these students by helping them to see that they can control their outcomes by their effort. This may require you to start off with very small steps so that the child can experience success. Then, take extra care to point out a specific action on their part which led to their success. It is also beneficial to praise them when they succeed, but don't go overboard on this. Children can easily detect false praise. A display in the room that publicly charts progress and effort is also an excellent way of assisting students in seeing the results of their efforts.

4. Help them to connect learning to life.

In order to be motivated, these children must see the utility of what they are learning. That utility must be of two types: utility to themselves and utility to the world around them. Provide activities where students can apply what they are learning. Encourage challenged learners to bring their own experiences and background into the learning situation. Get them out of the classroom as often as possible into real-world situations where they can see their faith and the power of God's Word in action.

5. Maintain high expectations.

Very often society's response to children who are low achievers is to give in and lower expectations. We place these students in programs where they are not expected to do much or where the standards are lower. Then, when they achieve no higher than those standards, our perceptions about them and their perceptions about themselves are reinforced. Many challenged learners did not learn the first time because the teaching methods used with them were inappropriate, not because expectations were too high. Yet, our tendency is to put the entire blame for failure on the student and recycle them through the exact same process again. We know that most people tend to function at the level expected of them. Maintain high expectations for challenged learners, but assist them in meeting those expectations.

6. Teach to a variety of learning styles.

We now know that not all students learn the same way. In fact, there are many different ways in which all of us learn best. Unfortunately, challenged learners often have learning styles different from styles valued and tapped in most classrooms. Many challenged learners need instruction presented in a way that gets them actively involved in practical "hands-on" activities. They also learn better visually and through tactile and auditory means. Challenged learners' failure to learn and respond appropriately is often not the result of their lack of ability. Rather it is due to differences in their style of learning. As Bible class teachers, we can help these students understand and achieve by varying our techniques and teaching to as many different styles and learning preferences as possible. This can be done by presenting instruction in several different formats as well as by organizing activities that tap into different learning preferences.

7. Use student-mediated teaching techniques.

One of the most exciting innovations in education is the use of student-mediated learning. These approaches are very successful in helping challenged learners achieve. Techniques such as Cooperative Learning and Peer Tutoring are particularly helpful. These approaches increase time on task, improve self-esteem and self-confidence, and teach positive social skills. Cooperative learning takes a variety of forms. Several variations have been developed which are particularly useful for at-risk students and students with special needs. In the same way, there are a variety of forms of peer tutoring that can be utilized. One form that has proven particularly successful is class-wide peer tutoring. This method is highly structured and requires the teacher to first instruct students in appropriate tutoring behaviors. These techniques will be explained in more detail in a later chapter.

8. Vary evaluation methods.

A good teacher, whether in an academic classroom or a Bible class, uses evaluation data to guide instruction. We are constantly assessing our students to see if they are learning and if our teaching is having the desired result. However, it is a fact that many students do not do well on paper and pencil tests. With these students we are not evaluating their knowledge as much as we are evaluating their ability to take tests. Use other ways of assessing these students that do not rely as heavily on traditional evaluation approaches. Some possible methods are demonstrations, discussions, observations, checklists, and products. By varying our evaluation methods we can more accurately discover what challenged learners really know and we can provide more opportunities for them to succeed.

9. Use positive, proactive behavior management strategies.

One of the most common complaints about challenged learners is their behavior. While there have been many types of discipline programs and approaches developed, the fact is not one program or approach is going to work with all students, or even consistently with the same student. Equipping yourself with information and skill in many different techniques will increase your chances of dealing successfully with behavior management problems. The best approach is to be proactive by developing a classroom environment that discourages the development of inappropriate behaviors. Teachers who have positive classrooms where all students feel accepted, valued, successful, and where all students clearly understand behavior expectations and consequences, have much fewer behavior problems. This will also be addressed more fully in a later chapter.

10. Be aware of the time factor.

Time is an important part of the learning equation. Time is content specific. It takes us longer to learn some things than it does to learn other things. We know that not everyone learns everything at the same rate. Unfortunately, in most classrooms we allocate to all students the same amount of time for learning a specific skill. Allowing all students sufficient time to master a skill may mean that you will need to vary the amount of time allocated to different students. Some may grasp the skill quickly and be ready to go on to something else. Other students may need to spend additional time before they have achieved mastery.

> **Teachers who have positive classrooms... have much fewer behavior problems.**

Another way that time can be of help with challenged learners is in response time. Many at-risk and special needs students have difficulty with language. It takes them longer to process questions and develop answers. As teachers we are often impatient when we don't get an instant answer and we either supply it ourselves or ask someone else to respond. This causes the challenged learner to think they are not capable students, when that may not be the case at all. One of the greatest gifts you can give challenged learners is the gift of time. Try allowing at least five seconds for a student to respond. Or, perhaps cue them in advance that you are going to call on them and give them a little time to prepare a response. It may make all the difference in the world.

Many of us have experienced the frustration of trying to teach challenged learners. What we must remember, though, is that these children also experience frustration every day of their young lives. By incorporating these ten principles into the fabric of your Bible class you can change children of challenge into children of promise. In so doing, you can help them to realize their potential and embrace their future.

Speak Up, Speak Out

Select one student in your class who is having difficulty learning, behaving in an appropriate way, or forming productive social relationships. Write four things that you will do over the next month to help this student.

_____

_____

_____

_____

Select one lesson you often teach in your Bible class. List at least three different ways in which you can evaluate students' mastery of that lesson.

_____

_____

_____

Think of a well-known story from the Bible, such as Jesus' visit with His parents to Jerusalem when He was a boy, or David's victory over Goliath. List the different methods you might use to teach that story thinking about all the different learning avenues: visual, auditory, kinesthetic, and tactile. Describe what the activity would look like using each of these avenues of learning.

_____

_____

_____

_____

Lift Your Voice

Lord, give me patience and wisdom to see each child as an individual and to find the key that opens the door of knowledge for all my students.

Grant me, O God, a creative mind to create a classroom that is successful for everyone.

Our Brains Are Different

In Mark 2 we read about a young man who could not move his body because a part of his brain did not work well. His friends, though, helped him to get near Jesus. Sometimes when part of a person's brain doesn't work the way it needs to, he or she must learn other ways to do things. Having supportive friends can help!

BRAIN PUZZLE
PUTTING OUR HEADS TOGETHER

Each part of your brain helps your body do something. Sometimes, when people are very sick or when they have been in an accident that caused a head injury, parts of their brain do not function smoothly. They may have trouble doing an activity that's controlled by the injured area of the brain.

- Color the picture of the brain below (use different colors for each piece).

- Then glue the brain to a thicker piece of paper.

- Cut the brain apart along the dotted lines.

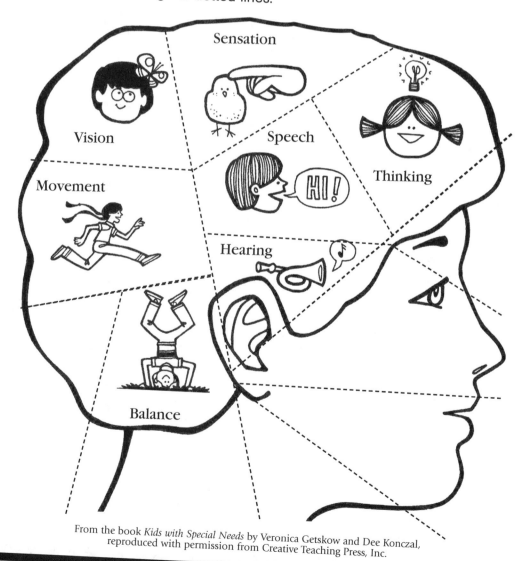

From the book *Kids with Special Needs* by Veronica Getskow and Dee Konczal, reproduced with permission from Creative Teaching Press, Inc.

More Alike than Different

All of us have more things in common than we have differences. We can build on our similarities to develop friendships and relationships. Your students, regardless of their abilities, disabilities, or backgrounds, will share interest in many of the same hobbies, games, sports, holidays, and other activities.

Have the children in your class draw and label a poster of things they like. If necessary, help young children, or children with more severe disabilities, label their pictures. When drawings are finished, have kids exchange posters or find other kids with the same likes. Let them discuss what their posters say about themselves.

Be sure to stress the activities described rather than focus on the quality of the children's artwork.

5

Disabilities and Strategies for Success

While labels can be overused and abused, they can also be helpful in understanding and categorizing disabilities. Knowledge of some of the major disability categories and their more common characteristics can assist Bible class teachers in planning and implementing more appropriate interventions and teaching strategies. In this chapter we provide a brief overview of the most prevalent disabilities you are likely to encounter in a Bible class.

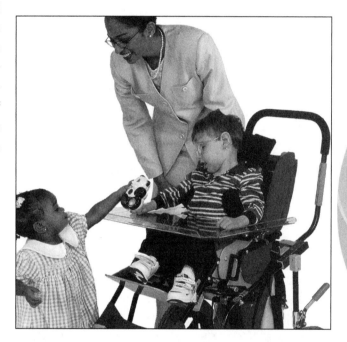

But Samuel said, "How can I go? Saul will hear about it and kill me." The LORD said, "Take a heifer with you and say, 'I have come to sacrifice to the LORD.' Invite Jesse to the sacrifice, and I will show you what to do. You are to anoint for me the one I indicate." Samuel did what the LORD said. When he arrived at Bethlehem, the elders of the town trembled when they met him. They asked, "Do you come in peace?"

Samuel replied, "Yes, in peace; I have come to sacrifice to the LORD. Consecrate yourselves and come to the sacrifice with me." Then he consecrated Jesse and his sons and invited them to the sacrifice. When they arrived, Samuel saw Eliab and thought, "Surely the LORD's anointed stands here before the LORD."

But the LORD said to Samuel, "Do not consider his appearance or his height, for I have rejected him. The LORD does not look at the things man looks at. Man looks at the outward appearance, but the LORD looks at the heart." **—1 Samuel 16:2–7**

God does not see or judge people in the same way that humans do. Thank goodness! When we look at others, we look upon their appearance first. It's as if we can't help ourselves. When a well-dressed, well-groomed child walks into our class, we are likely to make decisions about his intelligence and his success. These decisions usually correlate with that child's appearance. So what about the child whose appearance is tattered? What about the child who is in a wheelchair? For those children who look differently than "normal" children, we make decisions about them too. The decisions we make about these children usually correlate with their appearance. Sad but true. But there is good news in this story. The passage in 1 Samuel tells us that God looks beyond our outward appearance and straight into our hearts.

During the time of Samuel, no one was more shunned from society than the blind, the lepers, the paralyzed, and those who were deaf. In those days, "names" were used to categorize these people and to separate them. It is important that we use names to increase our understanding. In this chapter we will discuss a variety of children who have been given names for the purpose of increasing our understanding of their needs.

If the story in 1 Samuel suggests anything to me, it says this: If we use "names," we must not use them in making decisions about what we can and cannot do. Furthermore, we must not use names or labels to define a person's capacity to have a relationship with God.

A young lady by the name of Sarah lives in an institution nearby. She has lived there most of her life. Sarah has multiple disabilities including severe cerebral palsy and mental retardation. Her limbs are atrophied (withered) from years of no exercise. Looking at Sarah is almost painful.

In spite of her physical and mental limitations, however, Sarah can communicate some basic needs and wants by using an electronic communication board that is attached to her wheelchair. She can point to the picture of a bed. When she presses the button, an electronic voice says, "I'd like to go to bed now." Sarah can also request her favorite drink (coffee) and her favorite television shows. On Sarah's communication board is a picture of a cross. Anytime Sarah or one of her guests presses the button with the cross on it, the song "Amazing Grace" begins to play. Sarah's demeanor changes: her eyes light up; her mouth opens wide; and although she cannot sing, she vocalizes through a wide-open smile. Her body moves back and forth in her chair. It is clear that Sarah loves sharing her faith with others. Anyone who has witnessed Sarah's expression of her faith is blessed.

So what's in a name? Sarah has cerebral palsy and mental retardation. Cerebral palsy limits her physical mobility and mental retardation limits Sarah's intellectual functioning. What do these labels mean for a child like Sarah? They do mean that a child like Sarah wouldn't be able to do pencil and paper tasks. But they don't mean that a child like Sarah couldn't enjoy and learn in a Bible class. How would we minister to a child like Sarah in a Bible class? Perhaps we could sing to her or have the other children in the class sing to her. Later, we could create a small book containing pictures that represent different songs so Sarah could choose the songs she wanted to sing. In almost every class, there is a child who is drawn to children like Sarah. Identify those children and allow them to spend time with Sarah, reading and singing to her.

We must keep in mind that labels should only be used to help us understand better how we can include the child with a disability in our church. We should never use a "name" to exclude a child from those places where she learns about God's love.

The Experts Speak

Below is a discussion of some of the more common disabilities children in your classroom are likely to have, as well as a description of each one's learning and behavioral characteristics. Keep in mind that not all students with these disabilities will exhibit all of these characteristics. There is great variability in the characteristics of persons with disabilities. We must consider each child as unique.

The "expert" information found in this section largely comes from the National Dissemination Center for Children with Disabilities (NICHCY). This organization publishes copyright free information. You can get more detailed information at their website www.nichcy.org.

 ## Mental Retardation

Mental retardation is a term used when a person has certain limitations in mental functioning and skills such as communicating, taking care of him or herself, and social skills. These limitations cause a child to learn and develop more slowly than a typical child. Children with mental retardation may take longer to learn to speak, walk, and take care of their personal needs such as dressing or eating. They are likely to have trouble learning in school. They will learn, but it will take them longer. There may be some things they cannot learn. Mental retardation is not a disease, nor should it be confused with mental illness. Children with mental retardation became adults; they do not remain "eternal children." They do learn, but slowly and with difficulty.

Attention. The importance of attention for learning is critical. A person must be able to attend to the task at hand before he or she can learn it. Often attending to the wrong things, many people with mental retardation have difficulty allocating their attention properly.

Memory. One of the most consistent research findings is that persons with mental retardation have difficulty remembering information. Researchers have found that memory tasks requiring deeper levels of processing—those that are more complicated—are even more likely to show disparities between persons with retardation and their non-disabled peers than are memory tasks requiring shallow levels of processing—those that are less complicated.

Self-Regulation. One of the primary reasons that persons with mental retardation have problems with memory is that they have difficulties in self-regulation. Self-regulation is a broad term referring to an individual's ability to regulate his or her own behavior. For example, when given a list of words to remember, most people rehearse the list aloud or to themselves in an attempt to keep the words in memory. In other words, they actively regulate their behavior by employing a strategy that will help them to remember. People with retardation are less likely than their typical peers to use self-regulatory strategies such as rehearsal.

Metacognition. Closely connected to the ability to self-regulate is the concept of metacognition. Metacognition refers to a person's awareness of which strategies are needed to perform a task and the ability to use self-regulatory mechanisms. Those mechanisms may include planning one's moves, evaluating the effectiveness of one's ongoing activities, and checking the outcomes of one's efforts. Self-regulation is a component of metacognition. Persons with mental retardation have difficulties in metacognition.

Academic Achievement. Because of the strong relationship between intelligence and achievement, it is not surprising that students who are mentally retarded lag well behind their typical peers in all areas of achievement. Students who are retarded also tend to be underachievers in relation to expectations based on their intellectual levels.

Social Development. People with mental retardation are candidates for a variety of social problems. They often have problems making friends and have poor self-concepts for at least two reasons. First, many do not seem to know how to strike up social interactions with others. This difference is evident as early as preschool. Second, even when not attempting to interact with others, people who are retarded may exhibit behaviors that "turn off" their peers. For example, they engage in higher rates of inattention and disruptive behavior than their typically developing classmates.

Motivation. Many of the problems pertaining to attention, memory, self-regulation, language development, academic achievement, and social development place persons who are retarded at risk to develop problems of motivation. If these individuals have experienced a long history of failure, they can be at risk to develop learned helplessness—the feeling that no matter how hard they try, they will still fail. Believing they have little control over what happens to them and that they are primarily controlled by other people and events, some persons with retardation tend to give up easily when faced with challenging tasks.

Pervasive Developmental Disabilities (PDD)

There are five types of Pervasive Developmental Disabilities. These five known disorders are (1) Autistic Disorder, (2) Rett's Disorder, (3) Childhood Disintegrative Disorder, (4) Asperger's Disorder and (5) Pervasive Developmental Disorder/Not Otherwise Specified (PDD/NOS). Most parents and professionals are familiar with the term PDD as it is the umbrella term which encompasses each of these disorders. The five disorders in the PDD spectrum have many common characteristics. These children have impairments in social interaction, play, and communication. They have limited interests and their activities tend to be repetitive. These children do not relate well to others. Sometimes this includes their family members which can be devastating.

PDD spectrum disorders can be mild with the child exhibiting a few symptoms. Other children may have a more severe form of the disorder and have difficulties in all areas of their lives. It is important to know that Pervasive Developmental Disabilities present a very wide range of diversity. A single child seldom shows all the features at one time.

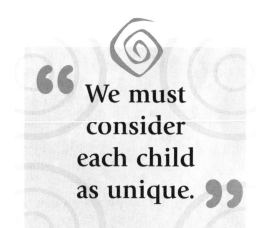

We must consider each child as unique.

Infants with one of the PDD spectrum disorders may:
- avoid eye contact.
- demonstrate little interest in the human voice.
- refuse to put up their arms to be picked up in the way typical children do.
- seem indifferent to affection.
- seldom show facial expression.

Young children with one of the PDD spectrum disorders may:
- continue to show a lack of eye contact.
- passively accept physical contact.
- approach a stranger almost as readily as they do their parents.
- show a lack of interest in being or playing with other children.
- avoid other children.
- use echolalia—a seemingly meaningless repetition of words or phrases.
- show unusual responses to sights, sounds, smells, and touch. Some children are under-responsive in such a way that their parents believe they are deaf. Other children may scream endlessly at the sound of a lawn mower two blocks away—a sound that you and I can't even hear.
- have great difficulty in accepting changes in routine.

Learning Disability

Learning disability is a term that describes a child who has trouble learning and using certain skills. Often these skills are reading, writing, listening, speaking, reasoning, and doing math. Children with learning disabilities are not "dumb" or "lazy." These children usually have average or above average intelligence. Their brains just process information differently. Learning disabilities are very common. In fact, it is likely that you have a child with learning disabilities in your Bible class because one out of every 5 people in the United States has some type of learning disability.

There is no single sign that a child has a learning disability. Experts look for a noticeable difference between how well a child does in school and how well he or she could do given his or her intelligence. When children have learning disabilities, they:

- may make many mistakes when reading (silently or aloud).

- may not understand what they read.

- may have messy handwriting.

- may struggle to express ideas in writing.

- may have trouble remembering the sounds that letters make.

- may have trouble hearing the slight differences between words ("pan" and "man").

- may mispronounce words or use a wrong word that sounds similar.

- may have difficulty organizing what they want to say.

- may not be able to retell a story in the right order.

- may become frustrated and easily embarrassed when they are required to "perform" according to the same standards we have set for other children (e.g., reading scripture aloud).

▶ Attention Deficit/Hyperactivity Disorder (ADHD)

ADHD is one of the most commonly diagnosed disorders of childhood. Children who have ADHD show inappropriate levels of inattention, hyperactivity, and impulsive behaviors. This is not the child who fidgets because he is bored. From time to time, practically all children can be restless, fidgety or impulsive. Children with ADHD have difficulty paying attention, sitting still, keeping their hands to themselves, and keeping their mouths closed whether they are at home, school, or church.

Children with ADHD are often blamed for their behavior. However, this is not a matter of their choosing not to behave. (Now, there are those children who choose not to behave but we aren't talking about those children right now, except to say that many of the strategies we implement in our classrooms to help the ADHD child, will also help these children). Children with ADHD often exhibit the following symptoms:

- inability to pay attention to details.

- have difficulty paying attention to tasks—even play.

- do not seem to listen when spoken to directly.

- have difficulty organizing tasks and activities.

- may avoid activities that require sustained mental effort.

- may lose things that are necessary (assignments, pencils).

- are easily distracted.

- may squirm and fidget in their seats.

- may run about or even climb the furniture.

- have difficulty playing quietly.
- may blurt out answers before questions are finished.
- have difficulty taking turns.
- have difficulty delaying gratification.
- are emotionally charged (over-reactive).

Voices from the Classroom

So, how do these characteristics affect students in the classroom and impact the way they learn? Let's look at the disabilities we have already discussed and examine ways we can successfully teach these children.

The Child with Mental Retardation

Since 87% of children with mental retardation will only be a little slower than average in learning new information and skills, you will have similar expectations of the child with mental retardation to that of the typical child. Here are some tips for making your classroom an embracing and successful environment.

- Give the child frequent feedback. Praise when he or she does well.
- Find out what the child is learning at home and at school. Build on these strengths by applying these skills in your classroom.
- Assign this child a buddy. Help the other children in your Bible class to understand the meaning of service to others.
- Be as concrete as possible. In other words, show the child what you mean rather than just giving verbal directions. Use pictures and gestures as often as possible.
- Break an activity that has many tasks into small steps. Draw pictures of each step. Have the child do the steps, one at a time.
- Present information and instructions in small, sequential steps. Review each step frequently.
- Talk with the child's parents about what they want him or her to learn. Help the parents to understand that their child is loved and welcomed in your classroom.

The Child with a PDD Spectrum Disorder

As a general rule, children with a PDD spectrum disorder will have greater difficulty adapting to your Bible class than children with mental retardation. The reason for this has little to do with intelligence. In fact, some children with autism are known to have average and above average intelligence.

These children are dependent upon routines and predictability. They are easily confused by new things in their world. They are also fearful because the new environment may have things in it that cause them great pain (e.g., unusual lighting, unfamiliar noises etc).

In order for a child with a PDD spectrum disorder to be successful in your Bible class, you will want to:

- Provide structure. As the child enters your classroom, present her with a "schedule" of the day. Show her each step in the day's routine. A daily schedule might look something like this:

  - Song: Jesus Loves Me
  - Song: I Have Decided to Follow Jesus
  - Story: Jonah and the Whale
  - Activity: Make a brown paper bag whale
  - Memory Verse: "Jonah loved God and obeyed him."
  - Prayer

- Add pictures to the schedule if the child doesn't read. The pictures don't have to be artistic. They just have to be good enough to help the child predict the day's events.

- Keep in mind that children with a PDD spectrum disorder are very literal learners. If the story book you use shows pictures of Jonah with a red hair, a beard, and a blue robe, all the other pictures of Jonah you use should also reflect Jonah with red hair, a beard and a blue robe—anything else isn't Jonah. (In our class, Jesus has worn the same clothes for a very long time).

- Keep verbal instructions to a minimum. Children with autism tend to "overload" on verbal information. Too much talking will create sensory problems for this child.

- Provide a buddy. When children with PDD spectrum disorders are more severely involved, they may need a consistent adult buddy. (Using different buddies only adds to the confusion that the child experiences).

Finally, remember that the first time this child comes to your classroom, he will most likely be upset. His routine has been changed. Take him anyway! Assure his parents that he will be okay. When his parents arrive to pick him up, tell them at least one thing that the child enjoyed. If, on the first day, he didn't enjoy anything, tell his parents that you enjoyed having him and you have faith that things will improve. If the parents will consistently bring him each Sunday, things will improve as the child adapts to this new routine in his world. It will be important that you have another adult in the classroom that day and for a number of weeks after that until the child has settled into your routine.

The Child with a Learning Disability

Children who have learning disabilities have average or above average intelligence. Yet, they are often overwhelmed, disorganized, and frustrated in learning situations—including the Bible class. Learning can be a terrible ordeal when tasks involve memory, following multiple directions, oral reading, and pencil and paper tasks. These children have negative self-images because of their repeated experiences with failure. The Bible class teacher who requires oral reading of scripture or other texts, recitation of memory verses, and written work can set a child with a learning disability up for disaster. This doesn't mean that we can't expect a child with a learning disability to do these things. Children with learning disabilities can do these tasks, but they may need modifications to help them. Here are some suggestions:

- Give the child advance notice of his scripture reading for next Sunday. Send him home with a printed version of the scripture so that he can practice with his parents or a sibling. Rather than require him to read the passage from the Bible, allow the child to type and read the passage you sent home with him. It will be a much less difficult task than reading from the Biblical text where the words are small and surrounded by so much extraneous text.

- Give children choices about written work. For instance, some children might prefer to write a story about what they learned in Sunday school. Others might prefer to draw a picture about what they learned. The things children have been able to communicate when they are allowed to draw pictures have fascinated me.

- Find out what things the child enjoys. Many children with learning disabilities excel in music, dance, and art. Incorporate these ways of expression into your teaching.

- Give all children the chance to engage in your lesson. Children are not passive learners by nature. Those that do learn passively don't do so by nature. Rather, they have learned compliance—they are polite and capable of tolerating and learning by this method. For many children, especially those with learning disabilities, passive learning is difficult if not impossible. In order to participate successfully, these children must be actively engaged in the process of learning. Some researchers call this "child-centered learning." Engage children by asking them what they know before the story begins. Invite them to reflect on the story after it has been read. Ask their opinions. Ask how they felt. Ask how the lesson they heard today applies to how they will treat other children in school the next day.

- If children are required to read large amounts of text before next Sunday, consider using a tape recorder. Record the passage to be read and send the recorder home with the child.

- Give lots of positive feedback to the child. The child with a learning disability knows much more about failure than he knows about success. Keep in mind that in a Bible class, we cannot only teach God's lessons, but we also show God's love.

The Child with Attention Deficit/Hyperactivity Disorder (ADHD)

Medication is often very effective in children with ADHD. But medication alone is not the answer. All children with ADHD must also learn strategies that will help them to deal with the disorder. ADHD can cause significant inappropriate behavior. Some children are even aggressive or anxious. Here are a few tips for working with the child who has ADHD:

- Be very clear in your communication. Say, "I expect you to…"

- Make your Bible class predictable. Post the daily schedule for the child to refer to as often as necessary.

- When you do change the schedule, give the child with ADHD as much advance notice as possible.

- Have a simple system for storage and organization—where to keep such things as pens, crayons, paper, glue, etc.

- Use as many visual reminders as possible. Children with ADHD have difficulty remembering verbal directions. Sticky notes are great for this. Simply drawing a picture and writing a note that says, "I raise my hand before I speak" will help Jason to remember to take his turn appropriately.

- Learn to let some things go. Pick your battles carefully. You don't want to increase conflict and arguments for this child.

- Don't ignore good behavior. Catch the child being good and comment on it.

- Let the child know exactly what the consequences are for misbehaving or breaking the rules. Put the rules and the consequences into writing and structure a time for the child to refer to these at each meeting. DO NOT expect the child with ADHD to remember the rules and the consequences on his own!

- Don't argue with the child. When problems occur, stay focused on the task or the rule that was violated and the consequence that was promised. Later spend some time analyzing the problem. Were your expectations clear enough? Did the child understand what was being asked of him?

- Always be specific. For instance, if you tell the children to "pick up the room" after an art activity, the ADHD child may only understand that he is to move one or two things out of the way. What do you really mean when you say, "Pick up the room"? The child with ADHD will need to know exactly what you what him to do.

- Teach students to self-regulate their own behavior by setting goals, monitoring and reinforcing their behavior.

> **"Learn to let some things go. Pick your battles carefully."**

Speak Up, Speak Out

I hope the information and ideas in this chapter have helped you to envision a picture of how children with disabilities can be successful in your Bible class. This chapter in no way gives a complete picture of all the disabilities or of all the ways in which we can help a child with disabilities to be successful in church. It simply serves as a place to start.

To increase the chances for success, it is important that you use your voice to talk with the parents or a family member of the child in your class. Some questions and discussion topics you should always consider are as follows:

Does the child have any medical needs that you should know about? Anything from food allergies to seizures are important pieces of information that should be related to you.

Is the child taking any type of medication? If so, what is this medication used for?

Do the parents or family members use any modifications for communication or movement? Would they like for you to try to use these same modifications in your classroom?

What activities does the child enjoy? What activities does the child dislike?

Another important way to use your voice is to talk with the other children in your class. Part of the job we have as teachers of children with disabilities includes teaching the other children in our classes how to accept and include these children in their lives as well. Use your voice to teach the other children in your class that we are all unique creations. Talk to them about the fact that we all have abilities (and disabilities). Talk to them and demonstrate for them that including children with disabilities gives us a way to show our love for one another.

Lift Your Voice

Ask God to help you look past the physical features of other people. Ask specifically that He help you learn to look upon their hearts first.

Ask God to help you use labels as a tool for understanding, not as a reason to categorize a child.

Reading Helper

Many children can benefit when material is presented orally as well as visually. One way you can help these children, and give your other Bible class students a chance to serve, is by creating a library of audiotapes on lessons you teach your Bible class. You can ask for help in obtaining tape recorders. Help and provide some training to your reading helpers on how to read and record information. Use the form below to ask for volunteer children who enjoy reading and are good at it. You may want to periodically have some activity or occasion to recognize your helpers.

Reading Helper

Thanks for volunteering to be a reading helper for your classmates. Here are the details you will need to know:

Please read: _____

_____

from page _____ to page _____

Special Instructions:

Reading Helper

Thanks for volunteering to be a reading helper for your classmates. Here are the details you will need to know:

Please read: _____

_____

from page _____ to page _____

Special Instructions:

Are You Listening?

Some students have difficulty participating in class discussions because their lack of reading skills makes it difficult for them to get the information they need. It is helpful if you can set up a listening station somewhere in your Bible class. This is also an activity that the child can complete at home. In order to help the child be more accountable, a product should be required of him or her. Here are some ways you can include audiotapes in your classroom:

Strategy 1

- Ask the child to listen to a passage on audiotape while following along in the Bible or workbook.
- After a short session of the lesson, the child should stop the tape, write a key word or draw a picture in the sequence boxes on the next page.
- The child starts the tape again and listens to some more material.
- Have the child again stop at predetermined times to make a note or picture of what has happened or of important points.

Strategy 2

- Have the child listen to a prerecorded selection on an audiotape.
- Afterward the child should tape himself or herself while retelling the story.
- The teacher, a teacher assistant, or a peer tutor can listen to the tape to check on the child's sequencing and understanding of the material.

Strategy 3

- Have a volunteer (see the activity "Reading Helper") create an audiotape of the text passage but add an additional twist: at regular intervals in the reading, ask the reader to stop and include a question about the content. (You may want to have the reader number the question to keep everyone on track.)
- When the child who is listening to the tape hears the question, he/she should write the number of the question in the sequence box and answer the question with words or a picture.
- The child can then start the tape and listen to the next passage and question.

From the book *Practical Ideas That Really Work for Students with Dyslexia and Other Reading Disorders* by Judith Higgins, Kathleen McConnell, James R. Patton, and Gail R. Ryser, reproduced with permission from PRO-ED, Inc.

Let All the Children Come to Me

Are You Listening?

1

2

3

4

6

Modify Instruction to Teach to Strengths

O ne thing you must buy into as a teacher of an inclusive Bible class is that you can't do things in the "usual" way: you can't teach in the "usual" way; you can't organize your classroom in the "usual" way; and all your students won't learn in the "usual" way. Flexibility, creativity, imagination, persistence, and a positive attitude are all tools that will serve you well. Perhaps the greatest tool is the ability to look beyond what others might see in your students and the way they might seem to the world, and to see them as God does. God does not look at the outward appearance. Rather He sees us all, not as we are, but as we can be.

T hen the LORD said, "Rise and anoint him; he is the one." So Samuel took the horn of oil and anointed him in the presence of his brothers, and from that day on the Spirit of the LORD came upon David in power. —1 Samuel 16:12–13

David was an unlikely candidate to be a king, let alone a great king. He was young and inexperienced. There were many others who seemed to have more talent—to be better king material. But God does not look at the outward appearance. He is not blinded by the obvious. He saw something in David no one else was able, or willing, to see.

God saw hidden strengths and talents and He was able to help David identify and develop those talents. One strength God saw in David was a sweet spirit—a heart that was gentle, compassionate, and tender. That would not seem to be an important characteristic for a king—especially a warrior king. Yet God knew that it was David's ability to be touched deeply and emotionally that would make him Israel's greatest king—a person who one day would be known as "the sweet psalmist of Israel."

We see this same ability to identify and build on people's strengths in Jesus. In Andrew Jesus saw "an Israelite in whom there is no deceit." In Peter, He identified a person of action—someone who had trouble staying still and needed to be active and moving. Jesus saw someone with an amazing capacity to love in John. By recognizing and helping them build on their strengths, Peter became a bold proclaimer of God's Word while John became known as the "Apostle of Love." These two men might have spent their entire lives fishing quietly on the Sea of Galilee if Jesus had not helped them find and use their unique strengths.

One way Jesus helped each person develop his or her potential was by not treating everyone the same. Jesus understood that each person was a unique individual with different needs and different abilities. Thomas was a visual-tactile learner, so Jesus let him see and touch. Peter needed the despair of failure to understand the true power of faith.

It is not much different in our Bible classes. It is so easy to be misdirected by the obvious: the way a child looks, or talks, or acts. We can be too quick to make judgments, dismiss a child as not being reachable, and as not being worth our time or effort. We must look to Jesus who never gave up, saw each person as unique and special, and then did whatever was necessary to help everyone He met to become the person God created them to be.

When I first met Robert he was lying face down on the floor of the principal's office. A teacher's aide was holding him down with one hand and trying frantically to get control of his flailing arms and legs with her other hand. His piercing screams were drifting through the open window to the parking lot below.

Although this was my first time to see Robert, I had heard plenty about him. I had just moved to town during the summer to take a job as the special education director for the school district. During the last two months faculty and staff had stopped by my office to fill me in on Robert. He was eight years old and had been attending school in the district for the past two years. Robert had a number of problems and no one seemed to know what to do with him. He frequently flew into uncontrollable rages and was usually noncompliant with the simplest of requests. It was difficult to know what set him off because he was nonverbal, had a hearing impairment, and some level of mental retardation. His behavior kept the school from obtaining reliable test scores on him.

School district staff had placed Robert in every type of special program they had. He had been in a program for students with mental retardation, one for students with behavior disorders, and a class for students with hearing impairments. Nothing had come close to working. The classroom he was placed in for the coming year was going to be the school district's last attempt to try to educate Robert. To make the situation even worse, the district's relationship with the parents was extremely adversarial and contentious. The weekly meetings held between the parents and district staff were almost always hostile and stressful for everyone, with accusations and allegations on both sides. Most meetings ended with the parents yelling demands and threatening a lawsuit.

> " The key to our success with Robert was to identify his strengths and... teach to those strengths. "

It would be safe to say that I was curious to see this young man who had so many people in an uproar. That's why I had driven over to his school on the first day of classes. As I got out of my car, I heard loud wails wafting out the window and across the parking lot. Hurrying up the stairs to the principal's office on the second floor I was greeted by the sight of the red-faced, panting aide wrestling with Robert and the principal on the phone, desperately trying to call the parents to tell them to come get their son, again.

The situation didn't look good. I was beginning to question my decision to take this job. Then, as I observed the scene in front of me, it suddenly occurred to me that maybe the problem was that the school district staff, instead of trying to meet Robert's needs, was trying to make him fit into their needs. We were trying to teach Robert the way we wanted to teach him.

I decided that we all needed a time-out. I got the parents and the school district to agree to send Robert to a well-respected pediatric unit at a nearby university medical center. Over the next six weeks I kept in close contact with Robert's doctors and therapists at the medical center. They determined that most of Robert's problems were due to a very rare neurological condition involving his autonomic nervous system that made it impossible for him to control his moods and behavior most of the time. They developed and implemented a combined program of medication and teaching that appeared to be effective with Robert.

In the meantime, I had convinced the district that the reason we had not been able to meet Robert's needs was because we were trying to make him fit into the programs we had and insisting he be taught the way we wanted to teach him. The fact was that Robert was unique. All the "usual" ways of teaching didn't work with him. So, in collaboration with the staff of the medical center, and Robert's parents, we developed a program that incorporated methods that built on Robert's specific strengths. As a result, Robert began to blossom. Within a year he was making real progress. His school experience became much more productive and enjoyable for him and everyone around him.

Let All the Children Come to Me

Another benefit was that our meetings with Robert's parents became more positive and less stressful as we stopped arguing about what the district would and wouldn't do. Instead we focused on what we all could do to help Robert learn. The program we developed cost us very little. We simply used, in different ways, the resources we already had. The key to our success with Robert was to identify his strengths and to then modify our instruction and teach to those strengths.

Robert's story illustrates the fact that not all students learn in the same way. Some children need to have lessons read to them. Others need to touch and manipulate their materials. Still some children need more structure. Other children need less. Modifying and adapting instruction successfully for all students requires flexibility and creativity. Most of all it requires us to see that every child is capable of learning to use the gifts God has given him or her.

The Experts Speak

There are several important concepts that can be helpful in modifying instruction for children with disabilities in Bible classes. First, effective planning is essential. If special needs children are to be successful in the Bible school program it will not happen by accident. Time invested in careful planning will pay off in a more productive and enjoyable experience for everyone. Collaborative planning is especially important. If you teach as part of a team, all team members need to participate in the planning process. If you are not currently working with other teachers, you may want to enlist the assistance of others in your congregation who may have expertise, experience, or, at least an interest, in working with special needs children. An important resource that should not be overlooked is the child's parents. They will have unique and useful insights into their child's learning style and needs.

A second concept to keep in mind is to "think inclusive, not exclusive." Do your planning from the presumption that the child will learn and participate in the same setting as all the other children. Our traditional approach in teaching children with disabilities has been to separate and segregate the child. This has usually been done because it is easier and more convenient for the adults since we tend to focus on what the child cannot do, rather than what he or she can do. Such an approach leads to negative perceptions of the child's ability and potential. It leads us to conclude that he or she cannot be successful in the same setting as other children.

Such a method should be avoided. Everyone benefits when all children can learn, serve, and participate together. Rather than automatically assuming that the child with disabilities will need a separate program and setting, presume that the child will remain with all the other children. Then, ask yourself, "How can I modify the setting, activity, methods, etc. to allow this child to be included?"

A third important concept that is closely linked to the one above is to "build on strengths."

Instead of seeing the strengths, we often see only the weaknesses of the special needs child. When we look at someone with a disability we tend see the disability first. Sometimes that is all that we see. We look no further and make certain assumptions about the individual based either on what we see or the label he or she wears. The disability becomes a barrier that prevents us from seeing the strengths and gifts that lie beyond.

In fact, children with disabilities, any disability, have more in common with their non-disabled peers than they have differences. Consider the following descriptions. One focuses on weaknesses; the other on strengths.

> ## " Think inclusive, not exclusive. "

Kathy Kathy is a 13-year-old Bible class student who has Down syndrome. Her I.Q. is 52, in the moderate to low range of mental retardation. Her language skills, both expressive and receptive, are at the 5 1/2-year-old level. Her basic reading skills are very minimal. She has difficulty focusing on a task for a very long period of time. She does not follow oral directions well and needs almost constant supervision.

Lynne Lynne is a young teenager who likes being with other children her age. She is very friendly and out-going. She is very good at remembering details and learns well visually and can complete tasks that are part of the daily routine. She has a lot of curiosity and likes doing things independently. She enjoys looking at pictures, doing crafts and singing.

The interesting thing about the two examples above is that they are both describing the same person, Kathy Lynne. We get two very different views of Kathy based upon whether we focus on her weaknesses or her strengths. If we look at only the first description, we would wonder how she could possibly survive in a regular Bible class with her non-disabled peers. But, by reading the second description, we can identify a number of strengths that can be used to help Kathy Lynne participate successfully in a regular Bible class.

Voices from the Classroom

There are various ways Bible school teachers can adapt the classroom, as well as their curriculum, for special needs children. Remember that an important aspect of modification is careful planning beforehand. There are some basic steps that might be useful in guiding this planning process.

1. What is the class expected to do?

2. What can the child with disabilities do?

3. Can the child do the lesson as is?

4. Can the child do the lesson with different materials?

5. What level of adaptation is needed for the child with disabilities?

There are several reasons why curriculum modification can be problematic for some Bible class teachers and classrooms. The need for training is certainly a big issue. Another is the educational paradigm of many teachers which suggests that all students in a class must be working on the same thing, at the same time, in the same way, for the same reason. It is important that Bible class teachers change that paradigm. Children can actually work on a number of different levels within the same class. They can:

- work on the same task with the same materials (no adaptations needed).
- work on the same task, but an easier step.
- work on the same task, but with different materials.
- work on the same theme (objective), but a different task.
- work on a different theme, and a different task.

Some important guidelines to keep in mind when modifying an activity or assignment for a child with a disability are:

1. Focus on what the child can do.

2. Modify, adapt, or accommodate before changing the activity.

3. Use the least obtrusive support first.

4. Use age-appropriate materials, goals, and activities when planning how to adapt.

5. Not all students learn the same thing, in the same way, at the same time—AND THAT IS OK.

David Gaston, Olympia School District, Olympia, Washington, offers some very important questions to ask when modifying curriculum.

1. Can the student do the same activity at the same level as peers?

    IF NOT

2. Can the student do the same activity but with adapted expectations? e.g. less words.

    IF NOT

" How can I modify the setting, activity, methods, etc. to allow this child to be included? "

3. Can the student do the same activity with adapted expectations or materials?

   IF NOT

4. Can the student do a similar activity but with adapted expectations?

   IF NOT

5. Can the student do a similar activity but with adapted materials?

   IF NOT

6. Can the student do a different, parallel activity?

   IF NOT

7. Can the student do a different activity in a different section of the room?

   IF NOT

8. Can the student do a functional activity in another part of the building?

Remember to always move from inclusive to exclusive. In other words, assume that the child with disabilities will participate in all class activities with the other children. Any modification has the effect of excluding the child to some degree, so add modifications only when necessary and only to the extent necessary.

There are many ways that a classroom teacher can modify and adapt curriculum and instruction for the special needs student. The diagram below illustrates this.

In Chapter 7 we will talk more about behavior and ways to modify, adapt, and teach children with unique behavior needs. In terms of instructional modifications, though, remember to keep in mind the student's strengths. In our example above, for instance, it would be helpful to give Kathy Lynne a series of pictures that illustrate classroom rules or routines since her reading skills are poor, but her understanding and visual memory for pictures is strong. By using her strengths we can help her to accommodate for her weaknesses and she can be a happy, helpful, productive member of the Bible class.

Types of Modifications

Input Variations	Level of Difficulty
Output Variations	Support Needs
Alternative Goals	Active Participation
Size of Assignment	Alternative Curriculum
Extra Time	

Speak Up, Speak Out

In your Bible class today you have planned a lesson based on Jesus' Sermon on the Mount. You want to particularly focus on Matthew 6:33 where Jesus says, "But seek first his kingdom and his righteousness, and all these things will be given to you as well." You want the class to work in groups to discuss and produce a list of things that get in their way of practicing this admonition in their daily lives. Then they will create a plan for how they can implement Jesus' charge in their own community during the next month.

In your class you have a number of students with disabilities as described below. You are going to assign each of these students to separate groups consisting of three other, non-disabled, students. For each student with disabilities complete the planning guide following the student descriptions.

Kevin Kevin is a young man with mental retardation and cerebral palsy. He is very good at following routines and enjoys competition. He can walk, but has limited use of his hands. He likes listening to Bible stories and has a good memory.

Sylvia Sylvia is a student with mental retardation and a speech handicap. Sylvia's speech is limited and difficult to understand. She prefers verbal communication but will use a picture communication system if prompted. Sylvia can count objects (one to one correspondence) to 100 and reads on second grade level. Sylvia likes to write with pencils and markers.

Jason Jason is a student labeled emotionally disturbed with poor impulse control. He will often talk out in class, making inappropriate and irrelevant comments. While other students' outbursts tend to set Jason off, he is able to consistently sit at his desk and work for approximately 15–20 minutes at a time. Jason reads at the fifth grade level. He is a good artist and works at drawing for extended periods of time. Jason get easily frustrated when things don't go his own way and he may become verbally aggressive with others.

Joshua Joshua is a student with multiple disabilities. He visually attends to his environment and responds to social contact. He makes sounds to gain attention and answers yes/no questions by blinking his eyes. No one is sure of Joshua's cognitive abilities. Joshua is non-ambulatory and has limited use of his hands.

Russell Russell is a student with muscular dystrophy. He uses a motorized wheelchair to get around the school and is easily fatigued. Russell is extremely proficient on the computer. He requires a keyguard and an armrest to assist him when he gets tired. Cognitively Russell is an above average student who loves to listen to music, read, watch and play sports, and "hang out" with his peers.

Planning Guide

What is your goal for the special needs students in this assignment?

_____

_____

_____

How does each of the students participate in the assignment?

_____

_____

_____

Describe any needed modifications for each student.

_____

_____

_____

Lift Your Voice

Lord, give me a kind and collaborative spirit to work with my fellow teachers, parents, and others to provide the best Bible class I can for all my students.

Thank You, Lord, for giving me the opportunity to make a difference in the lives of my students and to help them grow closer to You.

Vocabulary Puzzles

Vocabulary puzzles can be used in a variety of ways to help students learn important names, events, or concepts in Bible class. They can be used in group work in class or in independent study. You can have puzzles in two parts with a word or name one part and its description on the other. Or, you can have them in three parts and include a picture clue as illustrated below. Another idea is to put the answer on the back of the puzzle piece for students to self check.

He put two of every animal on a big boat.

Noah

From the book *Practical Ideas That Really Work for Students with Dyslexia and Other Reading Disorders* by Judith Higgins, Kathleen McConnell, James R. Patton, and Gail R. Ryser, reproduced with permission from PRO-ED, Inc.

Do You Have a Clue?

1. Develop a list of Bible names or concepts (i.e. Paul, baptism, etc.).

2. Pair students up as partners.

3. Have one partner give clues while the other one tries to figure out the word.

4. Start off with general clues (5) and get more specific.

5. You can use the cards later to drill or quiz students.

6. For more variety, have students make up their own words.

7. For children with cognitive challenges, let them choose from several words to identify the correct one.

The word is _____

The Clues:

5. _____

4. _____

3. _____

2. _____

1. _____

The word is _____

The Clues:

5. _____

4. _____

3. _____

2. _____

1. _____

The word is _____

The Clues:

5. _____

4. _____

3. _____

2. _____

1. _____

The word is _____

The Clues:

5. _____

4. _____

3. _____

2. _____

1. _____

Planning Chart for Including a Child with Disabilities

How will _____ with a disability participate in the activity?

Describe any needed modifications in materials.

_____

_____

_____

Describe any modifications in services or assistance.

_____

_____

_____

Describe any modifications in structure or activity.

_____

_____

_____

What is your goal for the student in this activity?

How will you evaluate the activity?

7

Good Teaching Is Just Good Teaching

No special teaching techniques or strategies are going to be effective unless sound teaching practices form the foundation for your classroom. The truth is, most students, even those with disabilities, will learn and grow well in a classroom where the teacher uses effective strategies that are successful for all students. In

this chapter we discuss some good, basic instructional strategies that are appropriate for any classroom, whether you have students with disabilities or not. Once these practices are in place, additional, more specialized strategies may be used for those students who need them.

A *s he went along, he saw a man blind from birth. His disciples asked him, "Rabbi, who sinned, this man or his parents, that he was born blind?"*
"Neither this man nor his parents sinned," said Jesus, "but this happened so that the work of God might be displayed in his life." **—John 9:1–3**

This passage speaks to us in two ways. First, it suggests that, if we are not careful, we'll miss the point of teaching a child with a disability. We'll look upon this child as broken or incomplete and our relationship with her will be characterized by our giving and her receiving whatever it is that we have to offer.

No one is to blame. Her parents didn't do anything wrong (although it may take years for them to believe it). The first duty of her teachers is to look at her as a whole and complete child of God. The second duty is to convince her parents that we believe this is so. She is not a broken child. If anyone is broken it is her parents—and the reason is abundantly clear. Her parents have encountered so many people and situations where they were told—directly or indirectly, with words or actions—she did not belong. No one had to actually say anything to them (although many people have said far too much). It's the stares, frightened faces, and even the rolled eyes that express our deepest feelings. Her parents have seen them all. They know all too well the ways in which people express the sentiment, "I wish you would go somewhere else." And they do.

The second way in which this passage speaks to us is in Jesus' statement, "But this happened so that the work of God might be displayed in his life" (v. 3). Now that is big! God is at work in this child's life. It is our responsibility to see God in her life. Furthermore, we must keep that in mind when this child is behaving in such a way that we might be tempted to forget that she is a precious child of God with a ministry of her own!

Isn't it true that the successes we enjoy in life, work, and faith have come, at least in part, because someone acknowledged something in us that we, ourselves, had not yet observed? This is one of the ways we lift each other up in Christ. Why would we deny this observation in the life of a child with a disability? Reality is, she has as much to offer us as we have to offer her. When Christ is at the center of a relationship, we both give and we both receive.

The first step in good teaching is actually taken as a leap—a leap of faith that God's plan is unfolding in this child's life. The best teaching, then, is usually preceded by the question, "God, what is the lesson in this for me?"

I have worked with some of the finest teachers in the world. I have been blessed to work with great teachers in the public schools, at the university level, and through the work of King David's Kids. I wish that good teaching could be bottled and sold—I realize that saying that could raise some eyebrows. What I mean is that learning to teach, and teach well, is a complex process. I have seen teachers who demanded excellence in academics. Some children did well in their classrooms but others were emotional basket cases. I have seen other teachers spend a lot of effort tending to the emotional needs of their children at the risk of turning out children who don't function at their best academically.

"Good teaching is good teaching."

Then there are those teachers who make it all look so easy—even though we know it's not. These are the teachers who taught me that "good teaching is good teaching." I can't tell you how to become a good teacher (or a better one than you already are) without telling you about some of my experiences with these people. I would be remiss if I did not use our voice to tell you their stories   .

Alice   Alice is a first grade teacher. On the first day of first grade, Alice spends her entire day on one activity. Alice knows that before children come to school that they have been told, "When you go to first grade, you will learn to read." So that is what she does. It doesn't matter to Alice what background children come from. It doesn't matter to her whether children have mastered readiness skills from kindergarten. It doesn't matter that a child may have been identified as learning disabled or mentally retarded. All the children learn to read something on the first day that they arrive in her class. How does she do it?

Alice spends the entire summer collecting magazines and old picture books. She brings them to her classroom and as the children arrive she greets them, invites them to look at a magazine, and cut out pictures of things they like. The children glue these pictures onto a sentence strip that Alice has prepared which states, "I like _____." As the children glue their pictures to each page, Alice moves about the room, filling in the blanks for each child. Later in the day, children continue adding sentences to their story by completing the sentences, "I can _____." After lunch, the children compile their sentence strips into books with Alice's help and begin to read their books to one another.

At the end of the day, Alice informs the children of their first assignment. They are to take their books home and read them to their parents. Parents sign a form that says, "I listened to my child read tonight."

All children are successful in Alice's classroom. Alice doesn't view her children in groups of those who can and those who can't. She believes that all children will be successful in her class and they are. Furthermore, Alice doesn't become anxious about the curriculum that is to be taught in first grade. Many textbooks lie dormant on her first few days of class as she prepares her children for the world of first grade. She realizes that anything—whether it's first grade in public school or Bible school at your church—is that children believe they are capable by experiencing success first hand.

King David's Kids continues to grow. I thank God there is a place where families can come together to learn of His purpose for their lives and the lives of their children. At our meeting last month we grew by four new families. I must admit, however, that while I am grateful for this glorious opportunity for families, my flexibility and creativity is challenged from time to time.

As the new children entered our group, I noticed that one of the new children was particularly "high-functioning" for the group of children we currently serve. (Jeff) was an older child, very verbal, and especially concerned that we would think he was not smart. It was also clearly obvious that he and his little brother were going to be holy terrors. They hadn't been there five minutes and the house was coming down around us. We didn't have anything set up to meet this child's needs. What were we going to do? He didn't fit into this group.

Sherry I have already seen God's magnificent unfolding in my friendship with Sherry. I'm certain that He has sent her into my life for many reasons. Sherry must have seen the look of desperation on my face when she approached with her offer, "Do you want me to be Jeff's buddy tonight?" She didn't have to ask twice!

As Jeff and Sherry moved through each of the activities we had planned for the younger and "lower-functioning" children, I noticed that Sherry did an incredible job of "modifying up" for him. As I read the story to the group and asked basic questions, Sherry spent her time with Jeff asking him how he felt or what he thought would happen next. She then asked him questions about how he might apply what he learned to his life at school and with friends.

What I thought was going to be a disaster, turned out to be a very nice evening with the children—all the children.

Sherry and Alice have never met each other and yet they have so much in common. Neither of them has ever met a student she couldn't teach. Good teaching no doubt, takes a lot of skill, but it begins with the belief that everyone belongs, everyone has something to learn, and everyone has something to contribute. Sherry and Alice never view children as "broken." Rather, they understand that "this happened so that the work of God might be layed in [a child's] life."

The Experts Speak

Good teaching first begins with a belief—the belief that this child can learn, that in him lies the unfolding of God's plan. We must believe that his disability does not define who he is. Furthermore, he is not limited by that disability to the extent that the people in his life do not limit him. Once we arrive in this place, we are ready to move forward. That is the purpose of the remainder of this chapter.

The sections to follow in this chapter deal with ideas and strategies that we have found work with many children. Specifically, we will present ideas regarding cooperative learning, multiple intelligences, and the need for structure. Our goal is to offer you ideas that will improve the way your Bible class works, no matter what your situation. Whether you teach five children with autism in a segregated Bible class or you teach one child with Down syndrome alongside 12 "normal" children, our intent is to give you ideas that will support your teaching and improve the responses of all the children in the class.

Cooperative Learning

Using cooperative learning strategies enables teachers to include children with diverse abilities and needs into classrooms where they might not otherwise be successful. Cooperative learning is more than merely putting children into groups. Cooperative learning focuses on shared goals and outcomes. It is the instructional use of small groups so that students work together to maximize their own and each other's learning.

Cooperative learning works best when each child in the group makes a contribution. Not all children have to make the same contribution—that's the point of cooperative learning. Each child in a cooperative learning group will make the contribution that he or she is capable of making. In these small groups children will discover their own strengths as well as the strengths of others.

Cooperative learning works well because it allows us to teach a group of children with a diversity of backgrounds and needs. It also prepares children to become the adults we hope they will become. Children learn interdependence—something needed to be a positive family member. In cooperative learning groups, children learn to be individually accountable to the group. They feel a sense of personal responsibility toward the group's goals. Children also learn to use interpersonal skills: they must build and maintain trust, communicate effectively, and manage conflicts effectively.

Cooperative learning is a strategy that may not work well for children with severe disabilities. It will, however, work very well for children with mild to moderate disabilities. This is especially true for those children with low self-esteem since many children with mild to moderate disabilities struggle with self-esteem. Research on children with low self-esteem (Johnson, Johnson, and Holubec, 1990) found that these children tended to show low productivity, believe they will be unsuccessful no matter how hard they try, withdraw socially, and overreact to criticism.

When children are placed in "individualized" learning situations, they are isolated from one another's thinking. David Johnson (1990) and his colleagues have suggested that individualized situations can promote avoidance, apprehension, and even distrust of others. Cooperative learning, on the other hand, promotes the kinds of peer interaction that will promote acceptance through social support, higher-level reasoning, critical thinking, as well as improved behavior, motivation, and attitudes.

Generally, cooperative learning groups should range from three to six in number. Keep in mind that children do not instinctively know how the group is supposed to function. It is important that you tell the children exactly what is expected of the group(s). Remember to monitor the groups frequently. Nothing takes the place of your attention, direction, and input.

Next time, instead of giving the children individual pictures of Noah's ark to color, give small groups of children some brown paper, glue, markers, scissors, and some animal patterns. Tell the groups to create one Noah's ark for each group. Step back and enjoy the unending creativity and understanding of others that children never cease to demonstrate when they are in nurturing environments.

Multiple Intelligences

A number of years ago, Howard Gardner (1993) of Harvard University introduced the concept of multiple intelligences. Dr. Gardner suggested that children are intelligent in many more ways than we (adults) understand. In his book, *Frames of Mind*, Dr. Gardner demonstrates that there are at least eight kinds of intelligence. However, most of us only deal with two of them: linguistic and logical-mathematical intelligence. In other words, the child who reads, spells, computes, and reasons well will be successful. Many children are not so gifted in these areas, but they do have gifts. The other intelligences, according to Dr. Gardner, are musical, spatial, bodily-kinesthetic, interpersonal, intrapersonal, and naturalist.

How do the children in your classroom learn? In addition to the story the children will hear, provide the class with opportunities for imaginative or art activities, skits or short plays, songs, rhymes, or raps.

Learning Styles

Every child has a unique learning style. Although most children can learn material without serious difficulty, some children struggle more than others and may need the information presented in a different way.

Learning styles are driven by physiology as well as personality. For instance, some children are not able to read and think as well when they are in environments that use florescent lighting. Some children can think better when they are allowed to move about the room. Some children may learn best by working in groups, while others may prefer to work alone. Some children are equipped with high internal motivation. Other children need external rewards.

Tactile/Kinesthetic Learners

Children who learn through touch and movement obviously have their hands on everything: They enjoy moving about while reading; they rub their hands along the wall as they walk down the hall to your class; they can take gadgets apart and put them back together again and often bring those gadgets to Bible class with them. These children are often frustrating because they can't seem to keep their hands to themselves. They are often misinterpreted as being hyperactive.

Provide these children pictures to trace with tracing paper (e.g., maps, words, pictures from stories). Touch this child while you talk to him. Communicate your approval or disapproval through touching. Let this child help you make bulletin boards and class materials. When appropriate, let this child move about the room. Tactile/Kinesthetic learners enjoy using real objects, models, and manipulatives. They love "hands on" experiences.

Auditory Learners

Children who are auditory learners are inattentive to visual tasks. When they are given worksheets, they fiddle with them, shred the paper, or doodle on them. They don't enjoy art or drawing and they often don't enjoy coloring. Many children who learn auditorily rub their eyes. You may notice that they hold materials close to their face when reading. Sometimes they lay their heads on the desk when they work. The auditory learner doesn't always remember what he has read to himself, but he is likely to remember what he has discussed in class or small groups. They love jingles and songs and they enjoy talking.

These children learn through oral directions and do well when they are taught to talk through tasks. Use jingles, catchy stories, cheers, or songs to aid these children in mastery or retention of skills. They will be successful with puzzles, raised maps, globes. When using worksheets, make sure they are dark, clear, and easy to read. Allow these learners to read aloud. If you can find books on tape, allow them to listen to them instead of reading.

" Children believe they are capable by experiencing success first hand. "

Visual Learners

Children who are visual learners ignore verbal directions. They require a lot of repetition when it comes to asking questions and giving directions. Amazingly, these students may be able to sit in a noisy area without being distracted. You may notice that they are close observers of your face and lips. Once directions are given in class these children will watch others before they begin their work. They say "huh" often. They prefer art over music and may get lost in rote memorization. The visual learner often speaks too loudly and substitutes gestures for words. These learners dislike speaking before a group and do not like to listen to others. Visual learners can locate words quickly in the dictionary if they know the spelling but are completely lost if they must look up a word to determine the spelling.

Because this child's eyes are the key to learning, she must look at what she is to learn. Make every attempt to face these children when you speak to them. They need to see your mouth. Retention for what is read will be higher when allowed to read silently. Provide them with written directions. Allow older children to take notes as you present material or discuss issues. Give your oral instruction in small steps and with visual reminders. Ask the child to repeat what you have told him. Touch the child as often as possible, a hand on the shoulder, a pat on the back.

❯ Questions, Questions, Questions

Good teaching includes lots of questions, but not just any type of questions. You want to use questions that foster critical thinking, evaluation, and application. During your questioning process, be sure to allow "wait time" for children to process their thinking. Avoid yes-no questions. They lead nowhere and do not promote thinking or discussion. Also avoid the question, "Do you understand?" Replace it with the statement: "Give me an example so I know you understand."

Questions of Clarification
- What do you mean by...?
- What is your main point?
- Could you put that another way?
- What do you think is the main issue here?
- Can you give an example?
- Can you explain that further?
- Why do you say that?

Questions which Probe Assumptions
- What are you assuming?
- What could we assume instead?
- You seem to be assuming _____ . Do I understand you correctly?

Questions which Probe Reason and Evidence
- Why do you say that?
- Why do you think that is right?

- What would someone who disagrees say?
- What is an alternative?
- How are Mary's and John's ideas alike? Different?

Questions which Probe Implications and Consequences

- What are you implying by that?
- When you say_____ are you implying_____?
- But if that happened, what else would also happen as a result? Why?

Questions about the Questions

- Is this the same issue as?
- Does this question ask us to evaluate something?
- Is this question easy or hard to answer? Why?

Voices from the classroom

The Need for Structure

I must admit that I've learned more about the importance of structure from working with children than from reading research. At the risk of diminishing the contributions that many have made to this topic, structure is one of those things that may be harder to read about and apply than topics such as cooperative learning and multiple intelligences. Nevertheless, structure is extremely important to the success of many children with disabilities—from mild disabilities such as learning disabilities to more pervasive and severe disorders such as autism. Consider Mandy's story.

Mandy is a 7-year-old girl with autism. Mandy is very athletic. She loves the three hours she spends with me and my students once a month while her parents go out on a "date." Mandy's behavior, however, at the Gymnastics Center, is very different than on those Tuesday nights when she comes to the King David's Kids regular meeting. Consider these two very different scenarios:

Scenario #1

At the Gymnastics Center, Mandy enters. Her father removes her shoes. (No shoes allowed on any of the equipment). Mandy says "goodbye" to her parents as they leave and is escorted to the gigantic room where she will spend the evening with us. Mandy is allowed to leap into the boxes of foam, jump on the trampoline, swing on the rope, balance on the low beam—anything she wants to do.

We don't hear many words from Mandy in the way that we do on Tuesday nights at King David's Kids. Mandy is also prone to "self-stimulations." She stands with one foot in front of the other and, while bent at the waist, rocks back and forth. Sometimes she demonstrates this behavior while flapping her fingers in front of her eyes. Mandy is not easily re-directed. When one of the students suggests that she return to the trampoline, Mandy pushes away with a vocalization that would indicate, "I'm not happy about your suggestion."

Mandy enters the play area of King David's Kids. She is eager to be greeted by her assigned buddy (Mandy has the same buddy each week). In the playroom, Mandy usually chooses from three or four of her favorite play things. One of these choices is a secretary's type chair that spins. It is not uncommon to see Mandy in playtime laughing with her buddy and requesting to "spin me please." Soon after all the children have arrived, Mandy and the children in her group are shown a schedule with words and pictures. This schedule signals that it is time to transition to snack time. Although Mandy knows the routine well by now, her buddy sings to her, "What time is it? What time is it? It's time to eat a snack! Oh yes, yes, yes! Oh yes, yes, yes! It's time to eat a snack!" Mandy moves from the playroom to the snack room while her buddy sings to her. Following snack time, Mandy is shown the schedule again.

Scenario #2 Now it is time for Mandy and her group to go to story time. The transition is handled in the same way. Mandy moves to a different room while her buddy sings to her. Sometimes, Mandy sings with her. During story time, Mandy is presented with a Bible story. She sings songs that have been printed onto pages with pictures above the words. Although Mandy cannot yet read the words, she can read the pictures (symbols) above the words. Mandy's favorite song is, "He's Got the Whole World in His Hands." She enjoys pointing to the pictures as the song is sung and often engages in the hand motions as she and her buddy sing with the group. If I ask Mandy the question, "Who built the ark," Mandy may not answer. However if I sing the question as it is sung in one of our songs, "Who built the ark," Mandy will answer in the same cadence of the song, "Brother Noah built the ark." The smile on her face as she answers is unabashed.

It may not sound like I'm even talking about the same child, but that is the difference between Mandy in an unstructured situation and Mandy in a highly structured situation. If you saw Mandy for the first time at the Gymnastics Center, you might believe that her level of functioning is much lower than it really is. It really has nothing to do with her "level of functioning." It has everything to do with the fact that Mandy (like many other children with and without autism) responds much better to structure than she does to no structure at all.

How can you provide structure to your Bible class? It depends on the learners, of course. Mandy has autism and her needs will be different than those of the child who has a mild learning disability. But good teaching is good teaching and therefore, we can find some common themes in any classroom to help children be successful.

1. Post schedules for the class. Use words and pictures together for non-readers. Refer the children to the schedule each time there is a transition

(e.g., transition from singing to listening to the story).

2. Establish clear rules for routines and procedures. Post the rules and the consequences so that children can refer to them often.

3. Provide opportunities for children to participate actively and successfully. You can do this through providing a variety of activities—but do so within a familiar routine. Solicit student participation and provide time for them to respond to your questions.

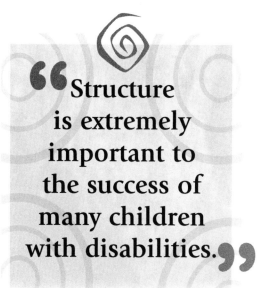

Structure is extremely important to the success of many children with disabilities.

4. Evaluate and give feedback to students during your teaching. Communicate your learning expectations and any expectations you have about specific behaviors. Remember to post these visually if needed. Monitor your students so that you can provide corrective feedback or clarification when needed. Don't just assume they are with you.

5. Organize your materials and your students. Get their attention before you begin. Use familiar procedures and routines. Give clear directions and maintain appropriate seating.

6. Use strategies that motivate children for learning the material or lesson. Tell stories which relate the lesson to children's lives today. Establish relevancy and purpose in the lesson. Provide an experience such as a field trip. Make positive personal comments every time students show evidence of interest.

7. Help children get started. Give familiar cues for beginning work. Give clear directions and provide immediate feedback.

Lift Your Voice

Pray that God will fill you with the belief that all children can learn.

Pray for each child in your Bible class by name. Acknowledge to God that in each child lies the unfolding of His plan.

Ask God to bring into your life, other people who can share their experiences and stories of success with children of challenge.

Speak Up, Speak Out

Is there room in your Bible class for the mechanical wizard, the child who dances well, or the child who performs skits brilliantly? Take a look at the following intelligences summary. See if you can identify the children in your Bible class who exhibit these various intelligences.

Intelligence	Enjoys	Strengths	Learns Best By
Linguistic	Reading, writing, telling stories	Memorization	Oral presentations, hearing and seeing
Logical/Mathematical	Doing experiments, figuring things out, asking questions, exploring patterns	Reasoning, math, logic, problem solving	Classifying, categorizing, reaching logical conclusions
Spatial	Drawing, building, designing and creating things, looking at pictures, watching movies	Imagining things, sensing changes, mazes or puzzles, reading maps or charts	Visualizing, working with colors/pictures
Musical	Singing, listening to music, playing an instrument	Remembering melodies, pitches, rhythms	Rhythm, melody, music
Bodily/Kinesthetic	Movement, touch, talk, body language	Physical activities (sports, dancing, acting) crafts	Touching, moving, manipulating objects
Interpersonal	Having many friends, talking to people, joining groups	Understanding people, leading others, organizing, communicating, resolving conflicts	Sharing, comparing, group problem solving, cooperative learning
Intrapersonal	Working alone, pursuing personal interests	Understanding self, following instincts, focusing inward on feelings	Working alone, self-checking activities
Naturalist	Working in nature, with plants and growing things	Harnessing nature to help others	True expression of the aesthetic qualities of nature.

Tips for Dealing with Difficult Behaviors from Children with Severe Sensory Impairments

Tantrums

Never respond to a tantrum unless the child's safety is an issue. By the time a tantrum occurs, it is too late to make attempts to calm the child. Instead, try covering the child with a lightweight blanket (to decrease incoming sensory information). Although you should always monitor these situations, try not to let the child see you watching her.

Running

Do not chase this child unless he is in danger. Set up boundaries in your classroom such as beads on the door. Bells on the door can also serve as an alert to you. These children often respond positively when you give them something to push (small grocery cart) or carry (large stuffed animal) and will be less likely to run.

Tactile Defensiveness (Resists being touched)

Continue to touch the child, but use deep pressure rather than a light touch. Deep pressure is more calming, assuring, and it helps to stabilize the nervous system.

Resists Sitting in a Chair

Turn the chair around and sit behind the child while the child straddles the chair. This will work during short tasks. Consider the floor for tasks that take more time.

Lack of Eye Contact

Bend at the waist when speaking to the child so that you are at his eye level. Leave only a few inches between the child's face and yours. Hold everything up by your face as you speak to the child. AVOID saying, "Look at me." Rather, animate the sound of your voice so that it catches the attention of the child.

Inappropriate Laughter

If you have ever experienced a child who uses inappropriate laughter, it can be a bit unnerving or even frightening. Ignore the laughter. After a few occurrences ask the child, "What's so funny?" When the child doesn't respond, tickle her and say, "Now that's funny."

In this activity you can review Bible characters with your students by having them complete a form like this on their own or in small groups. You may prefer to complete the form as a whole group activity by using an overhead projector or reproducing the form on a marker board.

Who is it?

The person was:

1. What was he or she?

2. What was he or she like?

3. What did he or she do?

4. What can we learn from him or her?

Books in Motion!

This is a wonderful way to help children remember the books of the Old Testament. It is a great strategy for all children, especially those who have difficulty with memorization, those with ADHD, and kinesthetic learners. Teach the children 4 or 5 book motions at a time and gradually build up until you get all the way to Malachi. As the children are learning the books make sure to tell them the meaning behind the motions. Later you can just say the book names and go through the motions! Get moving!

In the beginning there was nothing until God created the world. In Genesis we learn about how God got His wonderful plans started. When you say the name for this book begin by squatting down and then stand up while making a big sweeping circle with your arms to remember what God did in the beginning—Genesis!

Exodus tells us the story of how God used Moses to lead His people out of Egypt. When you say the name of this book make a "this way out" motion with one hand—Exodus!

In Leviticus God gives His people laws to live by. Salute when you say the name of this book—Leviticus!

In the book of Numbers God's people are counted. With the pointer finger of one hand, touch the fingers of the other hand like you are counting when you say this book—Numbers!

In Deuteronomy Moses tells the Israelites to love God with all their hearts. When you say this Bible book place your hand over your heart—Deuteronomy!

Joshua was a brave soldier who stood for God. Pretend to swing your sword when you say this book—Joshua!

God chose the judges to make decisions for His people. Touch one finger to the side of your head like you are trying to make a decision when you say the name of this book—Judges!

Ruth was a woman who was humble and faithful to her mother-in-law. God blessed her and gave her a husband to care for her. Curtsy when you say the name of this book—Ruth!

In First and Second Samuel we read about Samuel and King David. These were both men who listened to God. Put your hand up to your ear like you are listening when you say these two books—1st and 2nd Samuel!

In First and Second Kings we read about many different kings, some good and some evil, who ruled over Israel. Make a crown on your head when you say these books—1st and 2nd Kings!

A chronicle is the story of a place or a group of people. Some of you have read the Chronicles of Narnia. First and Second Chronicles tell many stories about God's people. Hold your hands like a book when you say these two books—1st and 2nd Chronicles!

Books in Motion!

   Ezra led God's people back to Jerusalem. Make a beckoning motion with your hands as though you are asking someone to come to you when you say this book's name—Ezra.

Nehemiah rebuilt the wall around Jerusalem. When you say the name of this book pound your two fists together like hammers—Nehemiah!

   Esther was a beautiful queen that risked her life to save God's people. Sweep your hand in a circle around your face to remember this beautiful queen (This is actually sign language for "beautiful.")—Esther!

Job had all kinds of problems. When you say this Bible book put the back of your hand on your forehead in a "woe is me" fashion—Job!

    The book of Psalms is a collection of songs to God. When you say the name of this book move your hands as though you are directing music—Psalms!

Proverbs are rules to live by. Shake your finger like a teacher saying, "Do what I say!" when you say this book—Proverbs!

In the book of Ecclesiastes we read that there is a time for everything. When you say this book's name point to your wrist like you are showing someone the time—Ecclesiastes!

  The Song of Solomon is like a love song from a man to the woman he loves. When you say this Bible book, pretend to stroke the strings of a harp—Song of Solomon!

When Isaiah hears the call from God he says, "Here I am! Send me!" When you say this Bible book point at your chest with your two thumbs—Isaiah!

Jeremiah was called the "weeping prophet." When you say this Bible book trace tears down your cheeks with your pointer fingers—Jeremiah!

 In Lamentations people cry out to God. When you say Lamentations, clasp your hands together in front of you in a pleading motion—Lamentations!

Ezekiel called the people to remember God and return to Him. When you say Ezekiel place your pointer fingers at your temples like you're trying to remember something—Ezekiel!

 Daniel prayed even when the king said he would be thrown into the lion's den. When you say Daniel, put your hands together and bow your head like you are praying—Daniel!

Through Hosea's life we learn that God is always waiting for us with open arms. Hold your hands out as though you are welcoming a hug from someone when you say this book—Hosea!

Books in Motion!

continued

Because God's people turned away from Him Joel prophesied trouble would come like an army of locust. But when they return to the Lord He will restore the "years that the locusts ate." Put your fingers beside your head like locust antennas when you say this book—Joel!

Amos says that God spoke to His people like a roaring lion because they had turned away from Him. Show your "claws" when you say—Amos!

Obadiah warns that Edom will soon fall. Raise your hands above your head and then bring them circling around each other to the ground as you say—Obadiah!

God told Jonah to go to Nineveh and preach. He did not want to go! And when the people of Nineveh repented and God forgave them, Jonah was mad. Fold your arms in front of your chest and make a pouting face when you say—Jonah!

Micah calls people to come to the mountain of the Lord so they can learn God's ways. Touch your fingertips together over your head to make a mountain shape when you say this book—Micah!

Nahum reminds God's people that He is great in power. Make a "strong man" pose to remember the power of God when you say this book—Nahum!

Habakkuk complains to God because of the evil he sees around him. Place your hands on your hips and stomp one foot once when you say the name of this Bible book—Habakkuk!

Zephaniah says to be silent before God because the day of the Lord is near! Put your index finger in front of your mouth in a "quiet please" fashion and whisper the name of this book—Zephaniah!

The Lord told Haggai that the king of Judah would be like His signet ring because God has chosen him. Pretend to put a ring on your finger when you say—Haggai!

Zechariah prophesies that God will send a king to His people who will bring them salvation. The King will be gentle and ride on a donkey. When you say Zechariah put your hands out like you are holding onto reigns and bounce like you are riding a donkey—Zechariah!

Malachi is the last book of the Old Testament! You made it all the way through. Make a "safe" sign like a baseball umpire when you say the name of this book—Malachi!

8

Dealing with Difficult Behaviors

In order to establish effective classroom discipline, you must first define what you mean. When you hear the word "discipline," what is the first thing that pops into your mind? If you are like many people, you think about what you do when a student misbehaves. Discipline is often equated with punishment.

If that is all there is to discipline, the Bible class teacher is in serious trouble. There is very little in the way of punishment that is appropriate in the Bible class setting. Because of this, some teachers feel their hands are tied; that they have no options. This is particularly difficult with children who exhibit challenging behaviors due to a disability.

This chapter will address this issue. It is important to understand that a discipline plan begins long before a child misbehaves. It includes everything a teacher does in order to facilitate positive, appropriate behavior in the classroom. It is this definition of classroom discipline that will guide our discussion.

Fathers, do not exasperate your children; instead, bring them up in the training and instruction of the Lord. —**Ephesians 6:4**

Although this Bible verse refers specifically to life in a family, it can be applied to the classroom environment as well. As teachers, we have great power to frustrate or to empower. When a child does not behave in an acceptable way, we should ask ourselves: Have I done anything that might be exasperating this child? Have I set up a situation that is frustrating and therefore triggers precisely the behavior I am trying to stop? If the answer is yes, then we know who needs to change.

Consider the second half of the verse. In addition to providing an atmosphere that is nurturing and sensitive to a child's needs and frustrations, this verse calls us to view discipline as teaching. Very little of discipline is concerned with what we do to children when they misbehave. Discipline is primarily what we do for children to help them develop positive, healthy attitudes and behaviors.

I remember well the first time I became aware of this scripture. Sitting on my parents' bed with my two sisters for our nightly family Bible reading, I perked up when I heard my father read this verse. "What does exasperate mean, Daddy?" And so began a family joke that continues to this day.

From then on, my sisters and I took great delight in quoting this scripture for our dad. We could do this because my father already understood and lived this Bible verse. No, he wasn't perfect, but he and my mother understood that parents have great power to either make it easy for children to follow their guidance or to make it very difficult. They knew that it was their responsibility to establish an environment that minimized frustration and did not put "stumbling blocks" in the way of their daughters.

I love that our Lord is sensitive to the needs of children. He takes very seriously the call to welcome and teach children. Remember that the Lord Himself said that His own yoke is easy and His burden is light (Matt. 11:30). I am compelled to ask myself, "Is the yoke in my classroom easy? Is the burden that I am asking the children to carry light?" As the grownup in the relationship, I must be willing to make adaptations so that the children the Lord has placed before me do indeed feel welcomed and not frustrated. I can hear Him saying to us, "Teachers, do not exasperate your children; instead nurture them in the training and instruction of the Lord."

I was fresh out of college and starting my first teaching job in Miami, Florida. It was hard to believe, but I was going to be a second grade teacher. I was feeling mighty grown up and was determined to be a great teacher.

My children were few in number, 12 to be exact, but from seven different countries. They were from Columbia, Cuba, Jamaica, Japan, Puerto Rico, Guatemala, and, of course, the United States. It was quite a collection of cultures. Many of their parents did not speak English. I was to be their teacher. What was I thinking?

In that class was a little boy named Steven. He learned much slower than the other children and was often distracted. But these things didn't frustrate me. I knew he couldn't help it and I was patient as I dealt with these challenges.

Before you begin to believe that I was the perfect teacher for Steven, I have to tell you the rest of the story. Steven did have one behavior that drove me crazy! He would turn in his papers with big holes all through them. I would repeatedly tell him to take better care in his work and still the papers would come in with holes.

One day I had simply had it! "Steven!" I said in my sternest, not at all nurturing teacher voice, "You must stop turning in your papers this way. There is no excuse for this!" Steven looked down in embarrassment and simply said, "Yes, ma'am."

It would have ended this way if not for Timothy, Steven's faithful friend. Timothy spoke up and said, "His hands sweat!" I then reached down and took Steven's hands in mine. They were dripping with sweat. I learned later that he had a metabolic condition that caused his hands to be wet all the time.

Needless to say, I felt horrible. I gave Steven a big hug and told him how sorry I was. We experimented with different ways to keep his papers dry and finally discovered how to fold a tissue under his hand while he worked. From that day on, Steven always had a box of tissues by his desk.

This encounter taught me some important lessons. First, I should never just assume that a child knows better or can do better. Sometimes children have challenges that make it difficult, if not impossible, to do what I am asking.

Second, if I am not willing to provide the appropriate supports to help a child be successful, then I have no right to punish the child for the behavior. Steven was seven. He didn't know what to do about his papers. He was just as frustrated about it as I was and I added embarrassment to this frustration.

I won't claim that I have lived these lessons out perfectly since then. However, they are principles that have guided my interactions with children in classrooms for over 20 years. I try to remember that all behavior has a reason and children need my support more than my reprimands.

Wherever you are, Steven and Timothy, thank you for this powerful lesson. I am sorry that I didn't know better before.

The Experts Speak

Any children with disabilities exhibit inappropriate behaviors in the classroom. These behaviors are often secondary results of the original disability. For some children a language disability makes it difficult for them to process instructions. Limited language can also make it difficult for a child to positively express needs or emotions. Other children have cognitive challenges that make it hard for them to read the social cues in the environment. Heightened sensitivity to sensory input may cause a child to be explosive in overly stimulating environments. Distractibility will often cause a child to disengage during instruction.

Whatever the cause, these behaviors can be very challenging. Barbara Kaiser and Judy Sklar Rasminsky (2003) have written an excellent book on this topic entitled *Challenging Behavior in Young Children: Understanding, Preventing, and Responding Effectively*. In their book they define challenging behavior as any behavior that:

- interferes with children's learning, development, and success at play.
- is harmful to the child, other children, or adults.
- puts a child at high risk for later social problems or failure.

This definition calls us to consider how the challenging behavior is affecting the child rather than primarily focusing on how the behavior affects us. Kaiser and Rasminsky remind us that, more than anyone else, the child would like the situation to be different.

Challenging behaviors prevent children with disabilities from learning important skills and concepts. They often impede the development of friendships and a sense of belonging in a group. The behaviors cause children to be denied access to settings and experiences that would enrich their lives and provide them with the joy of community. Instead, these children frequently find themselves rejected by their peers. They become isolated and are denied opportunities to practice and develop the social skills they desperately need.

These are serious concerns for all teachers, but of particular concern in the faith community setting. In the faith community we want everyone to find a place to belong. However, the behaviors exhibited by some children make this a very difficult task.

Often these behaviors are very persistent. When children persist in a behavior, it is because that behavior is serving some purpose for them. However effective or ineffective, the child uses the behavior to communicate many messages, including:

1. You are asking me to do something I can't do.
2. I don't understand what you want.
3. I want something, and I want it now.
4. I'm bored.
5. I need some attention.

6. I am feeling embarrassed.

7. I am experiencing more stimulation than I can handle.

8. I am feeling threatened.

These are feelings that are common for all of us. However, children with challenges often lack the skills to respond appropriately to these feelings. Additionally, they are frequently unable to read the social cues in their environment that typically developing children understand. This leads to behaviors that can, at times, be quite extreme.

As we work with these children it is crucial to focus first on understanding the behavior—to try to identify the communicative purpose behind the behavior. In this way we can focus our efforts on assisting the child in developing more appropriate ways to express desires, needs and emotions.

The first step in helping children learn appropriate behavior is to make it less likely that they will feel the need to use the inappropriate behavior. The Division of Early Childhood (DEC), a national organization of professionals who work with young children with special needs, reminds us that by changing our behavior, we may prevent a child's need to use the negative or challenging behavior (http://www.dec-sped.org/positionpapers.html challengingbehavior).

"All behavior has a reason."

While this may sound like a way to simply avoid the problem, it is in fact a proactive approach. When a child repeatedly engages in negative behaviors, these negative behavior patterns become more strongly embedded in the brain making it even more difficult for the child to discontinue this problem behavior.

On the other hand, when teachers and parents establish environments that make it more likely that the child will behave appropriately, these positive behavior patterns become more and more stable. In this way we are helping children form new habits through opportunities to practice the desired behavior. Therefore, prevention is truly the best form of intervention.

A preventive approach requires that we know our children. There is no simple formula as we work to address challenging behaviors in our classrooms. Different children may exhibit the same behavior for completely different reasons. In order to respond appropriately it is important to attempt to identify the function of the behavior. What is the child trying to tell us? What need is the child attempting to meet?

It is very easy to let frustration take hold as we work with children who exhibit these challenging behaviors. Avoid letting your own negative emotions determine how you will respond. Remember to look at these situations as opportunities to teach and assist the child in becoming an accepted member of the classroom community.

Voices from the Classroom

As previously stated, the largest part of any good discipline plan is what you do to prevent misbehavior from happening. In this section we will describe some simple strategies which you can use to establish preventive discipline in your classroom. While some of these strategies will be implemented with one child in mind, you will soon find that they are often helpful to all the children.

There are many aspects of the Bible class environment that set it apart from other classroom situations. You have limited time with the children each week. In larger churches you might not know about the child's family. The kinds of consequences for misbehavior you can utilize are often limited. It is easy to believe that you simply cannot discipline effectively within the constraints of this unique setting.

For this reason, the strategies discussed here will apply in almost any setting. They are very flexible and practical. They do not require a great deal of training in order to use them effectively. And, as previously mentioned, they focus primarily on prevention.

Meaningful Learning Experiences

The planning of interesting and engaging lessons is a very important aspect of preventive discipline. Find ways to actively include students in learning. Make connections between the content you are teaching and their personal experiences. Build on their interests and their abilities. Teach utilizing a variety of learning styles.

For learning to be meaningful, students must be able to succeed. Repeated failure can cause a child to misbehave in the classroom. It is important to make appropriate adaptations for children with challenges in your classroom.

Momentum and Transitions

Student engagement depends on how smoothly teachers move from one activity to the next. It is imperative to minimize wait time. Good and Brophy (2000) warn that "when students are required to wait with nothing to do, four things can happen and three of them are bad: (1) students may remain interested and attentive; (2) they may become bored or fatigued, losing the ability to concentrate; (3) they may become distracted or start daydreaming; or (4) they may actively misbehave" (p. 131). Recognizing that transitions are often times when students will lose focus and misbehave, you cannot leave these times up to chance. Always think ahead.

A common transition that can be quite difficult is the distribution of materials for an activity. Plan ahead how you will distribute materials quickly. Will you distribute them before or after you give instructions? How will you use the time it takes to pass out materials? Perhaps you could informally review the lesson so far. Songs can also be a very effective way to keep children focused during these transition times. Older students might turn to a neighbor and share one thing they remember from the day's lesson.

If students are going to change locations in the room, you must ask yourself how you plan to facilitate this move. I often use a countdown from 10, telling the children where I want them be when I get to zero. Another effective strategy is to move children in small groups rather than moving the entire group at once.

For children with challenges these transitions can be particularly difficult. Many disabilities make it very difficult for children to discontinue an activity and begin a new one. If transitions are too abrupt or frequent children can become frustrated and even explosive. For these children it can be very helpful to give them a warning so they can prepare themselves emotionally. Let them know, specifically, what will happen next so that they can reframe their thoughts and actions in preparation for the change.

> **The largest part of any good discipline plan is what you do to prevent misbehavior from happening.**

▶ Clear Instructions

Confusion about how to correctly do an activity is another common precursor to misbehavior. Giving clear and concise instructions is a skill that requires thought and practice. As you plan your lessons, give specific thought to how you will explain activities to the children.

A common misconception is that more words make clearer instructions. In fact, the opposite is often true, particularly for children with attention or language deficits. Work on giving instructions in as few words as possible. Model the activity when appropriate so that children can see what they are to do. You might ask a child to restate the directions to check for understanding. For younger children, give instructions one simple step at a time, being careful not to overwhelm. Finally, provide visual support for your verbal instructions. Using pictures to support written instructions can be very effective. In this way you are not only making instructions clearer, you are helping your students develop independence as they learn to use the visual supports you have provided to guide themselves through the activity.

In an effort not to appear overbearing and negative, teachers often phrase directives as requests. "Can you come over to the carpet for our story?" "Would you like to sing our song about Noah?" Another common habit is to add an "okay?" at the end of the directive. Phrasing instructions this way implies that students are free to decline. While some students understand these implicit commands, many children with disabilities are not able to read the social cues required to understand this kind of direction. Clear directives given in a positive, confident, and respectful manner are much more effective. See the end of this chapter for some examples.

Clear Expectations

In order for children to do what we want, they must first know what behaviors we expect from them. It is important to clearly communicate behavior expectations and periodically repeat these expectations for them.

Children will be more likely to comply with our expectations if they understand the reasoning behind them. Clearly communicate to children why certain behaviors are important in the classroom. Be prepared to support the children as they learn to use these behaviors.

Finally, do not make assumptions. One dangerous assumption that teachers commonly make is "They know what I mean." Many children with disabilities are simply not capable of figuring out the unspoken rules of social settings. They need things very clearly presented to them. Words like "behave" mean very little to them. In fact, I remember a four-year-old once saying to her teacher, "I'm trying to be a haive, but I don't know what it is!" Clearly define what you expect. "Please walk in the classroom."

This is another area where children with challenges, and those without, can benefit greatly from visual supports. Picture symbol communication support systems such as Boardmaker® from Mayer Johnson (see examples below) provide a rich resource for providing this type of visual communication.

raise your hand   **sit**   **please be quiet**

Sign language is another way to bolster verbal communication. I often use the signs for words like "sit" and "listen" when directing children's behavior. Not only does this provide the children with a visual cue, but as they join me in making the sign they give themselves a physical cue as well. This can greatly assist them as they work to comply with my instructions.

Another dangerous assumption teachers often make is that students know how to use the behaviors they expect. This is a sure invitation for frustration—for you as well as for the child. Remember, many children with disabilities will often require explicit instruction and additional support to behave in ways that come naturally for their typically developing peers. You should model for your students the behavior you expect them to demonstrate so that they will know what it looks like. Then have them practice the behavior under your guidance until you are certain that they understand and are capable of performing the behavior.

I will illustrate this with an example I remember from my own teaching. Children with challenges often have difficulty defining personal space. They cannot set their own physical boundaries. I once had a little boy with autism in my class who had great difficulty in this area. He would often grab the other children's materials when they were working on an activity. This was very frustrating for the other children. Even when reminded to use his own materials, he simply could not tell when he had crossed the line.

I began providing the shallow flat boxes that sodas are often stored in to house his materials while he worked. This simple, inexpensive strategy defined the physical boundaries of the environment for him. He could see clearly where his workspace began and ended and was able to easily identify the materials that were his.

I was careful not to single him out in this process and provided the boxes for the entire class. As is often the case, an adaptation I made for one child proved to be helpful to all children. Not only did it define the workspaces, but it also made distribution of materials and clean-up more efficient.

Finally, avoid making the assumption that once they have been told what to do, children should always remember. Even with typically developing children, the excitement of the moment, fatigue, boredom, etc. can cause a temporary lapse of memory. For children with disabilities this will be even more frequent. Recognize and accept that you will need to provide gentle reminders for children. Learn to anticipate these times so that you can provide reminders before the behavior occurs. This proactive, positive approach will help you maintain a positive attitude about your children and about teaching. It will also contribute to the establishment of an emotionally safe environment for the children.

Routines and Procedures

Predictable environments are important for all children, but they are particularly important for many children with disabilities. Clear and efficient routines and procedures facilitate the development of a predictable environment. This is very important in order for children to feel emotionally safe in the classroom. When children feel unsure about what to do, they will often misbehave.

Think about your classroom. Do children know what to do when they arrive? Is there a predictable sequence of activities and structures to your class time? Are the same people there each time or does the personnel change frequently? These are all important aspects of a predictable classroom.

Many children with disabilities have a very strong need for predictability. One way to provide them with an additional sense of security is to display a picture schedule. Again, Boardmaker® is an excellent source for creating these supports. (See examples below).

story

pray

sing

These picture schedules can be displayed for the benefit of all the children. If there is going to be a change in the day's routine, such as a guest speaker, you can point this out ahead of time, adding a special picture to the display.

Some children also benefit from having their own individual picture schedule. They can then refer to this schedule throughout the class period. These pictures can be placed on a ring so that the child can change the picture as you move through your time together. Again, if there is going to be a change in the routine, prepare the child by providing a picture to represent this change.

Redirection

Teachers often feel they need to correct or directly address every behavior infraction. They will ask, "Don't children need to be disciplined when they break a rule?" This reflects the common misconception that discipline and punishment are the same things. The answer to the question is, "Yes, they do need to be disciplined." However, this is most often in the form of redirection.

If a child is shouting out answers without raising her hand, make eye contact and raise your hand as a gentle reminder. Physical proximity can be another powerful way to redirect children. Simply walking over to stand close to the child will often provide the support the child needs to change her behavior. When a child drifts off during a class discussion, casually address a comment directly to her, "Suzanne, look at this picture. How do you think this little boy is feeling?" It is important never to use this strategy to embarrass or "catch" a child. Your goal here is to subtly draw the child back into the lesson.

Correction

While prevention is your primary focus, there will be times when you will need to directly correct a child's behavior. There are some simple guidelines that can help you as you do this.

First, always do your best to correct student behavior in private. It has often been said that we should praise in public and correct in private. I think this is a wonderful guiding principle to remember.

As you correct behavior, it is more effective to tell students what you want them to do rather than what you do not want them to do. Children are also more likely to comply with initiating rather than terminating commands (Walker & Sylwester, 1998). Consider the following examples:

Terminating: Elizabeth, stop drawing on the paper.

Initiating: Class, put your crayons in the box on the table and put your hands in your lap.

Students often perceive terminating commands negatively. Also, many challenges make it difficult for children to stop a behavior. It is easier for their brains to process a start command instead. Work on using initiating commands whenever you can. It will take some practice, but it will be worth it. Students will be more likely to do what you have asked and it will contribute to developing a positive emotional tone in your classroom.

Celebrate Small Victories

As you work with children who exhibit challenging behaviors it is important to focus on progress and not perfection. Many students will continue to behave inappropriately despite your best efforts. Children who persist in negative behaviors can be very unnerving for teachers. You may begin to feel defeated and helpless. It is common to develop feelings of resentment or anger toward the student. Strain and Hemmeter (1997) challenge teachers to look for small progress with these children. They warn that a "never again" or "fixed for good" orientation will set you up for disappointment and frustration. Remember to celebrate where you are in comparison to where you were.

Concluding Thoughts

Perhaps you are a veteran teacher and these strategies have served to remind you of things you already know. Or perhaps you are just beginning to face some of the challenges we have talked about. It is easy to get overwhelmed and want to give up or to just want the child to be removed from your classroom. These feelings are normal. Classrooms are already very complex and dynamic places without children with challenges. Take it a step at a time. Choose one or two strategies that you believe will best fit your classroom and your teaching style. Practice them for a while until they become habit. Then come back and try some more.

Finally, when I find myself feeling extremely frustrated with a child, my tendency is to forget to pray about it. I believe that God wants all children to feel welcome and valued in His church. So, before you get to the point of frustration, commit yourself to prayer. I find that the most transforming prayer is not the one that focuses on God equipping me to deal with the child or that asks God to change the child's behavior. These are valid prayers to pray. However, God powerfully transforms my attitude when I stop praying "about" the child and start praying "for" the child. When I join in the will and heart of God asking that the child come to know and serve God fully, then I begin to see this "problem" in my classroom as the Lord sees her or him. And I remember that when I welcome this child I am welcoming the Father as well.

he first step in becoming an effective classroom manager is to know yourself. Many of the

Let All the Children Come to Me

Speak Up, Speak Out

The behaviors children use can trigger very strong emotional responses. It is easy to leave behind the ability to respond objectively and reflectively and to simply react based on how the child has made us feel. This is perfectly natural. The good news is that the God we serve can provide us with His perfectly supernatural Spirit to help us in these situations.

Get together with a fellow teacher. In the space provided below, write down the feelings you have had when the children you are in charge of misbehave. This includes both your own children and your students. Don't hold back. Name them all!

After you have made the list, think of times when these feelings have determined your response. Can you remember a time when you acted in haste and later wished you had done it differently? Perhaps there was a time when your response was more intense than the situation warranted. Don't be afraid of this. The fact that you have responded in this way simply means you are normal.

Finally, spend some time in prayer about this. Ask the Lord to direct your responses to children's misbehavior. Read Galatians 5:22–25 and use this as a prayer to invite God to lead you by His Spirit.

When my students misbehave it makes me feel:

_____

_____

Positive Phrasing

Children are more likely to comply with our requests when they are phrased in positive terms. In fact, some language processing challenges make it difficult for many children to understand negation. It is clearer for them if we tell them what we want them to do and not just what we don't want them to do.

When we just tell children what not to do we are assuming that they know the appropriate alternative behavior. This is often not the case, particularly for many children with developmental or learning disabilities. Take, for instance, the first example below. This directive doesn't tell children how they should move in the room. It just eliminates running.

Use the following directives to practice this phrasing strategy. Change each one to be stated into positive terms that communicate clearly what the child is expected to do. Work together with a friend. Then try this in your next class meeting. You may find that it takes some practice.

1. Don't run in the room.

2. You can't use the markers right now.

3. Don't yell out answers.

5. Don't take the book away from Jimmy.

6. Please don't talk while I am talking.

7. Don't write on the table.

8. Don't talk while I am reading.

9. Don't scream when we are singing.

10. Don't push in line.

"God powerfully transforms my attitude when I stop praying *about* the child and start praying *for* the child."

Lift Your Voice

Pray for God to nurture in you the fruit of the Spirit as you minister to children with challenging behaviors.

Ask the Lord to guard your heart from anger and frustration.

Pray specifically for any child with challenging behavior in your classroom right now. Ask the Lord to bless that child with His love and peace. Pray that the Lord will fulfill His plans for that child.

May I Have Your Attention Please!
Five Easy to Use Attention Getting Strategies

Post these in your room for quick reference

1. If you can hear my voice, clap two times. XX
    (A little quieter)
    If you can hear my voice, clap three times. XXX
    (Almost a whisper)
    If you can hear my voice, clap four times. XXXX

2. Clap a pattern and have the children repeat it. Do three to four different patterns getting quieter each time.

3. I say "Abra", you say "ham"
    (Teacher) Abra (Children) ham
    (Teacher) Abra (Children) ham

    Try other combinations like the following:
    "I will" and "follow"
    "God is" and "love"

    Make up your own combinations to go with your lesson.

4. Do this quick rhyme to help children settle down
    Clap   Clap   Stomp   Stomp
    Clap your hands. Stomp your feet
    Walk in a circle   Sit down
    Turn around. Take a seat.

5. Just start singing!
    If the children are focused on an activity and you need to get their attention to give new instructions or transition to the next activity, just start singing a familiar song. It works much better than using your speaking voice.

Classroom Checklist for Supporting Positive Behavior

___1. Have I established an emotionally safe environment?
Do I use intentional strategies to make children feel welcome and loved?
   Greet each child by name
   Give children classroom responsibilities?
   Establish classroom celebration rituals (birthdays, lost teeth, etc.)?
   Get on child's level when speaking?

___2. Do I have clearly defined areas in my classroom?
How have I defined the physical space?
   Group meeting time area?
   Small group activity areas
   Individual workspaces?

___3. Have I established a predictable structure in my classroom?
Do children know what to do, where to go, and what they need during the following times?
   Entering the classroom?
   Large group, small group, and individual instruction time?
   Dismissal and departure?

___4. Do I plan for transitions in my classroom?
Do I utilize the following strategies to assist children with transitions from activity to activity and place to place?
   Give a verbal warning to prepare children for transitions?
   Signals (playing a song, ringing a bell, clapping a rhythm, etc.)?
   Minimize wait time (have materials ready for quick distribution, plan for fast-finishers, etc.)

___5. Do I provide clear instructions for children?
   Support verbal with visual?
   Provide models when appropriate?
   Check for understanding before beginning?
   Phrase instructions in positive terms?

9

Community
in the Classroom

One of the most important characteristics of any successful group, whether it is a church, a Bible class, a club, an organization or a neighborhood, is that of community. In order for our Bible classes to be places where all students feel valued, significant, accepted, and successful, we, as teachers, must build a sense of community. This is especially important when some members of your

class have disabilities which interfere with their learning, their behavior, and/or their relationships. Although this is written as the last chapter in this book, the concept of community should be the first thing that all Bible class teachers should seek to develop and sustain in their class. In this chapter we will talk about the importance of community to the classroom and some ways we can insure that all our students feel that they are a part of a caring and supportive community.

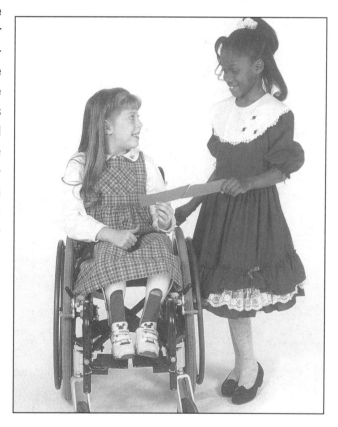

E veryone was filled with awe, and many wonders and miraculous signs were done by the apostles. All the believers were together and had everything in common. Selling their possessions and goods, they gave to anyone as he had need. —**Acts 2:43–45**

Community. It is a powerful concept and it was an important ingredient in the success of the early church. Jesus clearly understood the power of community. Between Jesus and His group of followers there developed strong bonds of love and commitment—bonds that were powerful enough to endure even his death. The first century church had a sense of community—when one hurt, all hurt, when one rejoiced, all rejoiced. Those who had much shared with those who had little. They had all things in common. This indicates interdependence and a shared responsibility. Over and over again we read in the book of Acts of the early Christians meeting to pray together, talk about common concerns, solve problems, and to support one another in whatever way they could, without ego, without competition. It was a mutually sustaining and nourishing relationship that always sought out the best in one another, built upon and used each other's strengths to overcome challenges and barriers.

This is even more amazing when we realize that the early church was composed of an extremely diverse group of people from many different backgrounds and cultures—a microcosm of society. The rich, poor, strong, weak, those with good social skills, and those without, those with many talents, and those with few—they were all part of the same community. They were family.

I experienced this same sense of community during the many years my family and I lived in areas where the church was not very strong numerically. Worshiping in small congregations and working in a highly secular job I remember the anticipation with which I looked forward to an opportunity to spend time with fellow Christians. I remember the joy I would feel when I would see a brother or sister through a chance encounter during a workday. We were family and we shared a special bond.

Just like the early church we were composed of many different kinds of people with different jobs, different backgrounds and experiences, but with a common faith, common values, and a common goal. We were part of a community who genuinely cared for one another and wished the best for one another, a community that would do whatever we could to help each member live a meaningful and joyful life.

Our Bible classes are, or should be, like that. They should be places where children feel nurtured, loved, and accepted—regardless of how they look or learn. Bible classes should be places where everyone is supported and encouraged; where we all accept responsibility for one another; and where one person's failures and frustrations diminish us all and each person's success enriches all of us. When challenges threaten, barriers block our path, and difficulties arise, it is our sense of community that carries us through and encircles its arms around us all. We are family.

When I first started teaching I worked with middle school students who had learning and behavior problems. Larry, a shy, very introverted, sixth grader, would not talk or interact in any way with the other students in the class. Every day when Larry came into my classroom for reading, he would crawl underneath the table and refuse to come out. Since I couldn't coax him into joining the reading group I started crawling under the table with him and we would have our reading instruction there. One day, Paul, a student with serious reading problems, asked me why I had reading with Larry under the table. I told him that was the way Larry liked to read. Paul asked if he could join us. I said, "Sure," and the next day Paul crawled under the table with us. A couple of days later we were joined by some of the other students. Soon, we were having our entire reading group under the table. Before long I noticed that Larry was beginning to spend time with the other students before and after class and on the playground at lunchtime.

" We are family. "

As the school year went by I began to see an amazing transformation among my students. I saw Larry begin to come out of his shell, to begin to initiate conversations in class, and to participate in group activities. He began to blossom and his social skills and self-esteem seemed to improve almost daily. At the same time, Larry, who was actually a pretty good reader, began to work during free time with some of the other students who struggled with reading. Their reading skills improved markedly. I saw a closely knit community begin to develop in our classroom. That class changed into a community of learners who accepted each other, unconditionally, who helped and supported one another, and who would not be satisfied until every member of the community felt accepted and successful.

While working on this chapter I was watching a news show early one morning. On this particular day they had a story about a young high school student, Eric, who has cerebral palsy. Eric's cognitive abilities are not affected by his CP, in fact, he is an honor student. Physically, though, he has limitations in getting his arms and legs to work well. While he can walk, his gait is slow and unsteady.

In spite of his limitations, Eric wanted to run cross-country. When it came time for him to enter high school his mother called the cross-country coach and told him that she had a son who wanted to be on the cross-country team. The coach said, "That's great." She replied, "There's a hitch, though, he has cerebral palsy." The coach told her that wasn't a problem and they would be glad to have him on the team. Soon Eric became a valued and highly regarded member of a community—his high school cross-country team. Although he never won a meet, his teammates considered him to be an important member of their community. Because he can only lift his feet off the ground a very small distance Eric would often fall six or seven times during a race, but would always get up and continue to run. When the other members of the team had finished running they would go back as a group, form a circle around Eric, and run the last mile with him.

That is community. It creates a supportive circle around each member, encouraging, lifting up, and joining together until everyone finishes the race. Community is a powerful force. We can talk about strategies, techniques, and programs, but the greatest resource any classroom has is community.

The Experts Speak

Elias, Arnold, and Hussey (2003) note that "the term 'sense of community' refers not to knowing the surrounding neighborhood, but rather to students' feelings of being cared about and influential in school and of being valued school members. In its emphasis on supportive interpersonal relationships, sense of community overlaps with the terms 'belongingness' and 'connectedness,' which are often used in the literature. But, it also reflects students' sense of 'voice and choice,' that is, their sense of influence and auto-nomy in the classroom and school at large." Elias, et al. go on to stress that bolstering a sense of community is one of the most important things a school can do.

The AbleNet Consortium for Excellence in Special Education (2004) defines community as a place where all students:

- experience a sense of belonging, caring and respect.
- have a growing network of meaningful relationships.
- look forward to each day because they have ongoing opportunities for relevant choices and shared fun.
- know that their voices and opinions are acknowledged and valued..
- experience an increasing sense of competence as they grow in awareness of their gifts and talents.
- know they contribute something unique, as they learn for each other.

How can a teacher develop a sense of community in the classroom? Elias, Arnold, and Hussey have identified four basic principles:

1. Build warm, stable, supportive relationships among and between students, teachers, and parents.

2. Provide regular opportunities for students to collaborate with others.

3. Provide regular opportunities for students to exercise "voice and choice" (i.e. influence and autonomy).

4. Articulate, discuss, and encourage reflection on core values and ideals.

Copple (2003) writes that the foundation for forging a caring classroom community must be mutual respect and communication. She notes that young children "need time to live through childhood egocentricity, immaturity, and inexperience before coming gradually to the point of regarding other people with interest and respect, assuming this is the ideal held by the adults around them." And Copple believes that the most important figure in this process is the adult role model. She writes, "Children learn to respect themselves and others, as they approach school age, not by our sermonizing or venting frustration with their naturally slow pace, but rather by our showing them what respect feels like and sounds like-by our showing respect for them, first of all." Joyce Eckes (2004) observes:

"I like to think about community as a verb. It is honoring every voice, creating ways for being and learning together, reaching out with respect and care, displaying everyone's work in the classroom, and nurturing each others' gifts and talents. It is creating fun and a sense of play, gathering and listening to each others' questions, telling and listening to stories from significant moments in each other's lives, celebrating the little things, sharing books, movies, experiences, and gaining courage as we learn and grow together. It is knowing that over time we are stronger for this and that we are not alone and that we are indeed part of something more and bigger than ourselves—something that makes living and learning a wondrous and beautiful miracle every day!"

> ## The greatest resource any classroom has is community.

Voices from the Classroom

So how can you develop community in your Bible class? An excellent resource is David A. Levine's book, *Building Classroom Communities* (see Resources). He provides some excellent activities to help build a sense of community in any classroom.

But, the process begins with you. If you want your students to develop a sense of community you must show them how. The first step is to model the concept of community to your students. The following guidelines may help.

- Show through your words and actions that you value every member of your class.

- Demonstrate respect in your relationships.

- Communicate to every child that you know he or she is unique and capable.

- Illustrate the idea of community by not being afraid to admit when you need help and support, be willing to accept the assistance of your students.

- Share with your students the difficult times in your life, as well as the triumphs.

- Let your students know that you appreciate them and that they are important to you.

- Set expectations for respect from everyone within your classroom.

> **The first step is to model the concept of community to your students.**

- Incorporate activities that focus on interdependence and shared responsibility rather than on overt competition.

- Give everyone in your class an opportunity to shine.

- Help your students to recognize and acknowledge the strengths in their classroom.

Try using the following activities to help your students understand the concept of community and to build accepting, caring, and supportive relationships in the classroom.

Lost in the Cave

All of us have unique gifts and abilities that can benefit others. This activity is designed to help students understand how everyone has strengths and limitations and how we can work together as a community to achieve common goals.

- Divide students into groups of four and assign the following roles: Reader, Chooser, Recorder, and Reporter.

- Using index cards have students write on three cards three things they are good at or that makes them special. On another card they write either a limitation they have, something they have difficulty with, or something they fear.

- Students put all the cards face down in a pile at each group's table.

- In each group the Reader reads the story, "Lost in the Cave."

- The Chooser selects seven cards from the group's pile.

- The group discusses how they can use the abilities from the cards selected to escape from the cave. When they come across a card that has a limitation or fear on it they are to discuss how they can use one of their strengths or abilities to lessen the impact of the limitation.

- The Recorder records the group's solution to the problem.

- The Reporter reports to the rest of the class the group's solution.

During an outing of their church youth group some children visited a state park. Four children named _____ , _____ , _____ , and _____ decided to go exploring in an old cave. They had been told to stay away from the cave, but it looked so interesting they couldn't resist. As they were exploring, they walked way back into the cave where it was very dark. They made several turns, exploring different passages. Suddenly they heard a loud noise behind them. When they turned to look they saw that part of the cave ceiling had fallen, blocking their way. They began to panic when suddenly they saw a small light coming from above them. This was their only hope, but they knew that the only way they could escape is if they worked together. They needed a plan.

Using the skills you have, how will your group escape from the cave?

Discussion:

What did you do to get out of the cave?

_____

_____

Do we all have things that we are good at and that can help us in difficult situations?

_____

_____

How do you make the best of a situation when you have to overcome your fears or limitations?

_____

_____

How do friends help each other build on strengths and minimize limitations?

_____

_____

Y O U R   V O I C E

Speak Up, Speak Out

An important part of the process of developing a classroom community is to first understand yourself. Either in a group or with a friend, share your responses to the following questions.

Can you think of a time when community was especially important to you? In what ways was it important to you? What were the bonds, the characteristics, which were formed and maintained in that community?

Think about the children that you have in your Bible class now. Is there a sense of community among class members? If so, what is it that makes the class a community?

If not, list below the barriers that you believe which are preventing the class from becoming a true community. Next, list the strengths in the class that you and the class can use to build a sense of community. Finally, list possible strategies you might use to transform your class into a caring and supportive community.

Barriers	Strengths	Strategies

In any community problems arise and disagreements develop. It is our respect and love for one another, our concern and caring for what happens to each other that continues to draw us together. Pray this week for each of your students. Ask God to help you develop a caring community in your classroom.

A Final Voice

The Eagle

The story is told of a black crow that stole an egg from an eagle's nest and deposited it in a chicken yard. When the baby eagle hatched, he looked at all the chickens surrounding him and he began acting just like them. He would scratch and peck in the dirt hour after hour, scratching and pecking day after day, just like all the chickens. As he grew, he never tried to spread his great wings and fly off, although he could. He never thought that he could be anything different than what he saw around him. He just spent his time like all the chickens, scratching and pecking in the chicken yard.

One day an adult eagle landed on the roof of the chicken coop. He watched the activity below him for a while and then spread his magnificent wings and flew majestically into the sky. The young eagle watched the adult eagle fly away and suddenly spread his own wings and followed, soaring gloriously into the heavens, following the adult eagle. When the young eagle saw his possibilities, he realized his potential. No longer would he be content to scratch and peck his entire life in the chicken yard. He was born for greater things. When he understood that, he became an eagle. He became what he was meant to be.

God has nestled in the heart and soul of every child the potential for greatness. Regardless of the way they may look, learn, or behave, God has created each and every one for noble and magnificent purposes. Yet, many children do not realize their potential because they do not see themselves as God sees them. You, as their teacher, have a unique opportunity to demonstrate to children that they are special because they were created individually and lovingly by a God who intended for them to live in His image. It is not necessary for them to scratch and peck in life's chicken yard. God has created them to soar majestically and gloriously. They just need someone to be their model, to show them the way. For some children the only champion, the only hero, they have is a teacher. It is up to each of us to help those children to see their possibilities and to understand their potential—and to become what they were meant to be.

Lift Your Voice

Lord, let me not be afraid to share my fears and weaknesses with others and to ask for their help.

Provide me, Lord, with opportunities to help others to bear their burdens and trials.

Show me, O God, that to change the behavior of others I must first change my own.

Belonging

Put students in groups of three or four and distribute one of the scenarios described below to each group. Have each group complete the following activities in regard to their scenario:

● Write an ending to your scenario.

● Develop a short role play illustrating your ending

● Present your role play to the rest of the class.

Scenarios

What if...Your family has moved to a new town and it is your first day in Bible class. You find that you are sitting next to Bob who uses a wheelchair and has trouble pronouncing his words clearly. After class you notice that Bob has no one to talk or play with him. What do you do?

What if...You know a girl (or boy) in your youth group is blind. You will be having a party at your house the next week and have invited your friends from church. What can you do to make everyone feel welcome and comfortable?

What if...There is a girl in your class who has trouble reading the Bible class story and has a very difficult time writing clearly. Some of the other children make fun of her. What can you do?

Lead your students through the following discussion questions:

Think of a time when you have felt left out, ignored, or different.

Describe how that made you feel. What emotions did you feel?

What did you think about the way you were treated?

What did someone do to help you fit in?

What do you wish someone had done (or not done)?

Share your answers with your group.

Bragging Buddies

1. Write brag phrases on cards. Focus on simple and fun ways for students to encourage one another. Put the cards on the students' desk or chair and put them on the wall where they are always visible. Start with two simple ones, "Good job" and "Good try."

2. When a student makes a correct statement, gets or does something correctly, students say "Good job." If the answer is not right, someone still offers a brag: "Good try." After students get the hang of it, gradually add other brags so that they have lots of choices. Some possibilities might include: Way to go! You can do it! Fantastic! You got it! I like that!

3. It is a good idea to let the students assist you in compiling a list that they want to use.

4. Make sure that all students praise each other. You can do this by passing out tickets at the beginning of the class, one for each student. After a student gives another student a brag, he or she puts a ticket in the jar and is qualified for the Bragging Bonus. The Bragging Bonus is randomly selected by drawing a name, which entitles the student to a reward chosen by the teacher and the student.

5. After every student comment, whether it's correct or not, students should reinforce each other with a brag.

After your students have become good Bragging Buddies, provide a few minutes every class or two to have them decide on the brags for the week.

Bragging Buddy

I am a Bragging Buddy.

Please enter me in the Bragging Bonus Drawing.

My name is

_____

Bragging Buddy

I am a Bragging Buddy.

Please enter me in the Bragging Bonus Drawing.

My name is

_____

From the book *Practical Ideas that Really Work for Students with ADHD: Preschool through Grade 4* by Kathleen McConnell and Gail Ryser, reproduced with permission from PRO-ED, Inc.

Quick Guide to Disabilities and Teaching Strategies

Attention Deficit Hyperactivity Disorder (ADHD)

Characteristics Children with ADHD have difficulty sitting still, controlling their behavior, and paying attention. They often have difficulty attending to details, organizing tasks or activities, and following instructions.

There are three types of ADHD:

1. Inattentive type. Child can't stay focused on a task or activity.

2. Hyperactive-impulsive type. Child is very active and often acts without thinking.

3. Combined type. Child is inattentive, impulsive, and too active.

Hyperactivity and impulsivity tend to go together. Children with this type of ADHD fidget and squirm, talk too much, blurt out answers, and have trouble waiting their turn.

It is easy to become frustrated with these children, so it's important to understand that they are not doing these things intentionally. Be aware that the problems these behaviors cause with peers and teachers can make these children feel anxious, unsure, and even depressed.

Strategies Because these children have difficulty organizing their world mentally, it is important to provide an environment that is uncluttered, orderly and predictable. Post rules, schedules, and assignments in the room. Establish clear routines; when things are going to change, let them know.

Provide appropriate ways to channel the child's physical activity. Allowing the child to stand rather than sit to complete an activity can give the child just enough movement to be successful. Whenever possible, integrate physically active and multi-sensory learning experiences into your lessons. Provide some kind of fidget toy (such as a squishy ball) for times when the child has to listen.

Give instructions visually as well as verbally. Step-by-step written or picture instructions can help the child get back on task after being distracted.

Distractable children benefit from having an uncluttered place to work away from the stimulation of the classroom. A computer can be another helpful tool to assist these children in focusing.

Most important, remember that these children get very frustrated and are often rejected. Be intentional about establishing positive, loving relationships.

Autism

Characteristics Autism is a lifelong neurological disorder which interferes with the development of reasoning, social interaction, and communication.

Children with autism have substantial problems with communication. About one-half of this population is nonverbal. Others may use language, but are very concrete thinkers and communicators with a limited ability to understand or express abstract ideas. They have great difficulty following spoken directions unless linked with visual supports. Many children with autism use what is known as echolalia, the repetition of words or phrases heard moments or even days earlier, e.g., Harry hears "Hi Harry" consistently when he enters the Bible classroom, so when he enters the room he says, "Hi Harry."

Children with autism vary in intellectual functioning. Mental retardation may accompany autism for some, while others demonstrate normal intelligence in some areas. Most children with autism have difficulties with learning and generalizing what is learned.

Strategies Structure and order are key components to success for the child with autism. The child with autism needs a routine that he can depend on each time you meet with him. Printed schedules accompanied by pictures (called social stories) are essential to this child's ability to integrate into your classroom.

Because children with autism respond better to information presented in visual form, the social story helps to stabilize the child in terms of what happens next.

They need to know that the experience in your classroom is going to be consistent and predictable. If they are confused, you will have problems. Tantrums are often the result of confusion. (Don't confuse this with the child who simply wants to have her way.)

When you speak to the child with autism, bend at the waist so that your face is at eye-level with his. While the child may not look directly into your eyes, he will be able to gather more information from you if you speak to his face. Other children are capable of look

Autism (continued)

Characteristics (cont.) A classic characteristic of autism is the avoidance of eye contact. Some adults with autism have reported that looking directly at other people is a somewhat painful experience.

The lack of communication skills often causes severe behavior problems. It also inhibits the understanding and expression of emotions. This results in a significant disturbance in social relationships. While attachment to people is rare, it is not uncommon for these children to develop excessive attachments to certain objects.

Children with autism almost always have one or more disturbance of the sensory system. Most often, these children have great difficulty in noisy environments. Other sensory stimuli such as light, color, odor, and texture can also cause problems for children with autism and impact their ability to learn.

Strategies (cont.) ing up at you while you talk, this child cannot; it will be necessary for you to make this compensation for him. Hold everything next to your face as you speak to the child. Avoid saying, "look at me." He can't.

Keep a set of ear protectors (the kind worn on a gun range) in your closet. Help the child learn to use them and always keep them in the same place in the room. The child will quickly learn to get them when he needs them and use them without your prompting.

Avoid light touches with children who have autism. Their sensory systems are often defensive and light touches such as pats on the back or stroking their hair can actually be painful experiences. Rather, use deep pressure when you touch them. A child in the middle of a tantrum may respond positively to very deep pressure (rubbing) on the back.

Bipolar Disorder

Characteristics "Bipolar disorder is a serious mental illness characterized by recurrent episodes of depression, mania, and/or mixed symptom states. These episodes cause unusual and extreme shifts in mood, energy, and behavior that interfere significantly with normal, healthy functioning." (National Institute of Mental Health)

When children with bipolar disorder are in a manic phase, they may be extremely irritable or overly silly and elated. They may also exhibit an over-inflated self-confidence and engage in risky behaviors. Manic symptoms also include increased talking and distractibility.

During the depressive phase, these children will often lose interest in activities they enjoy. They will show a loss of energy and may have difficulty concentrating. These children often feel worthless and may experience inappropriate feelings of guilt. It is not uncommon for these children to have thoughts about death or suicide.

Strategies It is very important to establish open communication with the child's parents. You might want to use a back-and-forth notebook to assist in this.

This child can benefit from having a one-on-one special assistant to help them participate positively in class, and to whom they may go if a "safe" person is needed.

The medications these children take can cause increased thirst or urination, so it is important to provide unlimited access to the bathroom and drinking water.

These children need a curriculum that engages their creativity and reduces boredom. Enrich classroom activities with art, music, and drama.

Avoid overreacting to the child's increased activity during manic periods. Ignore behaviors whenever possible and positively draw the child into appropriate interaction by providing opportunities to be involved in the lesson. When concentration is low, provide quiet activity options, such as reading a book or drawing.

Blind/ Visually Impaired

Characteristics There are several categories of visual impairment.

1. Partially sighted. Person has a visual problem that requires special assistance.

2. Low vision. Person has sight but cannot read the newspaper at a normal distance even corrected. These people will use a combination of vision and other senses to learn and may require adaptations such as a magnifying glass, enlarged print, or Braille.

3. Legally blind. Person has less than 20/200 vision in

Strategies Learn more about the extent of a child's visual impairment and their preferred mode of learning (large print, Braille, magnification, etc.) Work with the parents to make sure the child has access to the materials and resources needed.

When approaching or addressing a student with a visual disability, always state your name unless he or she can easily recognize your voice.

Describe for the student what others may see. For example, you may say, "I have made a chart to show

Blind/ Visually Impaired (continued)

Characteristics (cont.) the better eye or a field of vision less than 20 degrees. Totally blind children can learn only through Braille or other non-visual means.

It's important to remember that visual problems can involve not just acuity, but also field of vision and visual efficiency and functioning.

With some eye disorders vision may fluctuate from day to day or throughout the day during different lighting and environmental conditions. Even stable conditions may be influenced by lighting, fatigue, attention, and emotions.

Characteristics vary somewhat depending on the severity and type of the vision loss, age of loss, and overall functioning of the child.

Children with visual impairments tend not to explore interesting objects in the environment and, thus, may miss chances to gain experiences and learning. Their knowledge may be fragmented and incomplete because of their lack of visual information. Because they cannot see parents and peers they may not understand or imitate social behavior or nonverbal cues. Students with visual disabilities sometimes exhibit certain mannerisms, such as putting their fingers in their eyes, rocking, making extra or rhythmic movements, drooping their heads, or making inappropriate sounds.

Strategies (cont.) every student's classroom job. It has a list of jobs on one side and slots next to each job where we can put a card with the name of the student who is responsible for that task. Who can read the list of jobs out loud so we all know what they are?"

It's best to use whiteboards, and writing on board should be large. Read aloud information written on the board or overhead. Some students with low vision may need a copy of the notes you put on the board. Students may write large, but many, with practice, can reduce the size of their writing. However, they must be able to read it.

Provide a duplicate set of materials and have a classmate demonstrate the activity to the student at the same time the teacher is demonstrating.

Present a summary of key points from lectures in the student's preferred medium.

Allow the child to relocate in the classroom for different activities to enhance opportunities to see and hear.

Students with low vision may benefit from using a reading stand or another method for bringing the paper closer to their eyes. Special attention should be given to the clarity and contrast of enlarged copies.

Feel comfortable using words such as "see" and "look." Encourage the student to express his/her visual needs.

Cerebral Palsy

Characteristics Cerebral palsy is a term used to describe a group of chronic disorders impairing control of movement. CP is caused by faulty development of, or damage to, motor areas in the brain that control movement and posture.

Symptoms of cerebral palsy appear in the first few years of life and include difficulty with fine motor tasks (such as writing or using scissors), difficulty maintaining balance or walking, and involuntary movements.

The symptoms differ from person to person and may change, though generally do not worsen, over time. Some people with cerebral palsy are also affected by other medical disorders, including seizures or mental impairment, but cerebral palsy does not always cause profound handicap.

Because motor impairments often make their speech difficult to understand, people with CP are sometimes assumed to have mental retardation. While cognitive functioning may be impaired in some individuals, most people with CP have average or above average intelligence.

Strategies Focus on the individual child and learn firsthand what abilities and needs they have. Become knowledgeable about different learning styles and be flexible in using those that work best for a particular child.

Be inventive. Seek always to include the child with CP in all classroom activities. Ask yourself how you can modify/adapt the lesson for the child. If the child uses assistive technology, learn all you can about it and how it's used. It may be necessary to develop some "low tech" solutions to certain situations by adapting materials or activities.

The child with CP may need to use special equipment and furniture; allow room in your classroom if necessary.

Be patient. It may take children with CP longer than other children to do something. Wait for them. Talk directly to them and wait for them to communicate directly to you. It may take extra time and effort to understand their speech, but it's worth the effort. Use teamwork and community; let other students assist the child with CP in group activities.

Deaf/Hard of Hearing

Characteristics Sound is measured by loudness (intensity) and frequency (pitch). A hearing loss may be described as slight, mild, moderate, severe, or profound, depending on how well the person hears the intensities and frequencies necessary for speech.

In this regard, every person with a hearing disability differs, so it is important to find out more about what the child can and cannot hear. Individuals with hearing impairments also differ in how well they communicate orally (speech, reading, and speaking) and manually (sign language, finger spelling, gestures, etc.).

Perhaps the greatest difficulty most children with hearing disabilities have is their difficulty understanding and using the English language. The sign language used by most deaf people, American Sign Language, is very different from English.

The ability to use and understand English syntax and vocabulary depends on a number of factors, including the extent of the child's hearing loss (slight, mild, moderate, etc.) and when the hearing loss occurred (before birth, after birth, before or after language was learned).

A deaf student may act like they understand what you're telling them but in reality they may be confused, lost, and need further instruction.

Strategies The deaf student in the classroom will be relying on their residual hearing, speech reading (lip reading), your lesson preparations, and your visual and writing cues to understand the lesson that day. Seat the deaf student in a location where they can clearly see you, stay away from windows, never speak while turned away from the student (such as while writing on the board), and keep your hands away from your face.

It is also helpful to provide the deaf student with an outline prior to each class. Write a brief outline containing the major concepts on the board at the beginning of class for the deaf student to follow as you move from one topic to the other.

A deaf student may experience "classroom fatigue" faster than the hearing student. You may want to take periodic breaks and pause occasionally. Do not draw attention to their disability, such as making the deaf student read out loud or using the deaf student's hearing impairment as a way to keep the class quiet.

Consider assigning a buddy to sit next to them to fill in any verbal instructions they may have missed. If using an interpreter, talk to the child, not to the interpreter, and supply the interpreter with a copy of the lesson prior to the class.

Facial expressions, gestures, and other body language will help you convey your message.

Dyslexia

Characteristics Children with dyslexia demonstrate difficulty obtaining language skills at a level consistent with their intelligence. Despite average to above average intelligence they struggle with reading and spelling.

Because these children sometimes confuse sound similarities in language, their words may come out wrong or in the wrong order. At times they experience difficulty processing information and struggle to reproduce it in an understandable fashion.

Some children with dyslexia have challenges with organization. They may have difficulties with directions and often get mixed up.

These children may have good coordination except when using a pencil. Because of this, their handwriting is sometimes irregular, slow, and hard to figure out.

Even though they struggle with reading and writing, children with dyslexia often exhibit strengths in other areas. Many are gifted in areas of art, music or athletics.

Strategies These children perform best with multi-sensory learning. Find ways to explore stories and scriptures using many different senses.

It can be helpful to pair children with dyslexia with other children. This is especially true in situations that require reading and writing.

Make sure that materials provided are very clear and sequential. It can be helpful to provide picture cues along with written instructions.

Allow options for expressing understanding. Perhaps children can draw a picture or think of a way to act out the story or concept. If a computer is available, these children benefit from the option to use word processors. Do not make an issue of spelling. Emphasize content over neatness and spelling.

Because these children experience frequent frustration and embarrassment, it is important that use of these supports be invisible to the rest of the class. If picture cues and assignment options are provided for all the children, the child with dyslexia will not feel singled out.

Epilepsy

Characteristics Epilepsy is a physical condition that occurs when there are sudden, brief changes in brain cell function. Movement and consciousness may be altered for a short time. These changes are called seizures. Other things besides epilepsy can also cause seizures.

Characteristics of epilepsy may include:

•Blackouts or periods of confused memory

•Staring or unexplained period of unresponsiveness

•Involuntary movement of the arms and legs

•Fainting spells with incontinence followed by excessive fatigue

•Off sounds, distorted perceptions, unexplained episodic fears or feelings

Seizures can be generalized in which all brain cells are involved. This might result in a convulsion with a complete loss of consciousness. Another type looks like a brief period of fixed staring.

Seizures can interfere with the child's ability to learn. During brief periods of staring, the child may miss some of the teacher's instruction. Fatigue from seizures may require frequent absences from class. Children with seizure disorders are often on medication and the medication can have side effects.

Strategies Learn as much as you can about the child's disorder and history, including medications. Observe and document any seizures, large or small, and report them promptly to parents. Inform the parents if you notice any change in the child's personality, physical, or intellectual skills.

Stay calm if the child has a seizure in your class. Be sure to request and receive instruction in seizure management. This is not complicated or extensive, but important.

It may be necessary to break the child's work into smaller, more manageable pieces, and allow the child to rest occasionally. An adult or peer tutor may help the child catch up on work.

There are many myths, fears, and misconceptions about seizure disorders. Educate yourself about the facts and make sure the other students understand the facts, too. Treat the child as normal as possible.

Many people are able to keep their seizures to a minimum by avoiding situations that trigger them. Triggers may include lack of sleep, emotional upsets, or failure to take medication. Taking care of a child's overall wellbeing is a vital part of the complete management of his/her epilepsy.

Health Impaired

Characteristics This disability refers to any type of health problem that negatively impacts the child's educational performance. This can include a wide range of problems such as asthma, cystic fibrosis, diabetes, Tourette syndrome, heart conditions, etc.

The characteristics are as varied as the causes. Some are the result of the health problem itself and some the result of medications taken for the problem.

Some typical characteristics may include chronic absences, distractibility, poor organization, excessive fatigue, emotional and behavior problems, poor motor coordination, perceptual problems, slow working rate, lack of confidence, and poor social adjustment.

Children with health impairments may miss school on a regular basis, as well as other activities which may cause them to be somewhat delayed in academic and social skills.

Strategies Visit with the parents regarding the child's medications, abilities, and limitations.

Some types of health impairments make it difficult for the child to keep up with peers due to frequent absences, fatigue, or distractibility. These problems, as well as possible side effects from medication, may cause gaps in the child's knowledge and skills. A tutor, or buddy, may be helpful to the student, as well as adapting and modifying materials and activities. Present information in smaller amounts.

Check knowledge and understanding through verbal responses. Hold reasonable expectations for them. Don't foster overdependence.

Make provisions for any special equipment or assistance the child needs. Facilitate cooperative learning arrangements and activities.

Learning Disabilities

Characteristics The term learning disability is used to describe a child who has a significant learning problem in one or more of the basic processes involved in understanding or using spoken or written language. These problems may become evident in the child's writing, math, spelling, listening, and speaking skills. Children with learning disabilities have the potential to learn at their own intellectual level, but academic achievement is often below that potential.

These children make many mistakes when reading aloud. They often do not comprehend what they have read. Spelling and handwriting are difficult and many struggle to express ideas in writing.

Children with learning disabilities have trouble understanding jokes, comic strips, and sarcasm—any type of non-literal language. They have difficulty organizing what they want to say and they may not follow the social rules of conversation such as turn taking.

Strategies As with many other children, breaking large tasks into smaller steps is an effective strategy. Children with learning disabilities also respond well to a predictable, consistent routine and a well-organized environment. Use color-coding or highlighting to help them stay organized in your classroom. Use visual cues to assist your verbal instructions.

Summarize your material often. It is a good idea to have the children summarize the information periodically. Have them summarize in ways other than just verbal repetition (drawing, painting a mural, creating a shadow box, or presenting a short play).

Don't assume that this child knows the class rules. Make sure you review the rules with her—possibly at the beginning of each class—and post the rules somewhere in the classroom.

Mental Retardation

Characteristics Children with mental retardation have significantly lowered intellectual functioning. Deficits in adaptive behavior adversely affects their ability to learn at the rate of normally developing children.

Mental retardation is not a disease, nor should it be confused with mental illness. Children with mental retardation become adults; they do not remain "eternal children." They do learn, but slowly, and with difficulty.

People with mental retardation have difficulty in particular areas of basic thinking and learning such as attention, perception, or memory. Impairment may vary from mild to moderate, severe, or profound.

The great majority of people with mental retardation can become productive and full participants in society. Children with mental retardation are not emotionally impaired, but they may be immature. They are capable of learning, but retention of information they learn may be brief.

Strategies Make every attempt to teach children with mental retardation in the same classes with their same-age peers.

Be as concrete as possible. Demonstrate what you mean rather than just give verbal directions—show or draw pictures while you talk.

These children will respond best to hands-on materials and experiences. They enjoy the chance to try out things. Break long or new tasks into small steps. Demonstrate the steps. Have students do the steps, one at a time. Provide them with assistance when necessary.

Encourage independence in this child. While a peer helper or buddy may be helpful for this child, make sure that the buddy is not doing for this child what she could do for herself. If the other children in your class have chores, she should have chores as well. Keep her age, attention span, and abilities in mind.

Because retention of information may be brief, reteaching is essential.

Speech and Language Disorders

Characteristics Speech and language disorders refer to problems in communication and related areas, such as oral motor function. These delays and disorders range from simple sound substitutions to the inability to understand or use language or use-tion, autism, or cerebral palsy.

Characteristics of speech or language disorders may include:

Strategies The best instruction for these children will involve hands-on activities. Provide these children with a variety of experiences, using consistency and repetition. Divide your lessons into small units with the same theme.

Whenever possible, break large goals down into simpler sub-tasks that are easy for the student to accomplish. Be sure the child has mastered the

Speech and Language Disorders (continued)

Characteristics (cont.)

•articulation errors

•voice impairment

•disfluency

•inadequate social skills

•difficulty with verbal and written communication

•poor short-term memory

•academic difficulties

The child with a speech or language disorder may appear to you as the child who rarely talks, or conversely, as the child who can't seem to stop talking.

Children can have expressive or receptive language problems, or both. In an expressive language disorder the child has trouble expressing him or herself orally, or in writing. With a receptive disorder, the child may have difficulty understanding directions or processing information given orally or in writing.

Strategies (cont.) simpler sub-task before progressing to the more difficult one.

Offer opportunities for social interaction.

Use tactile and visual cues when speaking; when you ask questions allow some "wait time" for their response. Often, they need more time than their normally developing peers to formulate verbal responses. This is particularly true for children who stutter. Be patient as they struggle in their verbal responses. Do not show an expression of concern or pity with your face and do NOT tell the child to "slow down" or "start over." It is not helpful to say, "Think about what you want to say." Rather, allow the child as much time as he needs to formulate his response to you. Respond to him as you would to the child who does not stutter.

Give this child verbal and tangible reinforcements. As with all children, demonstrate patience, respect, and understanding.

Resources

Videos: Inclusion

Bittersweet Waltz, VHS. Produced by Linda Safan. Available through National Down Syndrome Society, 666 Broadway, 8th Floor, New York, NY 10012-2317. (800) 221-4602; fax: (212) 979-2873. A 17-minute video about inclusion designed as an educational tool for parents seeking to have their children included in a regular elementary classroom. Presents inclusion from a visual point of view, with some on-camera discussion. The feelings and insights of classmates are poignant.

Choices, VHS, DVD. Produced by Comforty Media Concepts for the Illinois State Board of Education, Department of Special Education. Available through Comforty Media Concepts, 2145 Pioneer Road, Evanston, IL 60201. (708) 475-0791; fax: (708) 475-0793. A thorough introduction to the philosophy and practice of inclusion. This video presents four personalized stories about how inclusion has affected the lives of people with disabilities, including people with Down syndrome. Interviews with families, friends, classmates, and coworkers provide a thoughtful means of addressing the multifaceted nature of the inclusion process.

Educating Peter, VHS. Produced by T. Goodwin and G. Wurzburg for HBO. Ambrose Video Publishing, Inc., 145 West 45th St., Suite 1115, New York, NY 10036. Awarded the Academy Award for Best Documentary Short Film in 1992, this thought-provoking film follows a child with Down syndrome through a year of inclusion in a public school. The film raises many questions about inclusion by honestly presenting the reactions to, and methods of, dealing with Peter's behavior problems.

Families, Friends, Futures, VHS. Produced by Comforty Media Concepts for the Illinois State Board of Education, Department of Special Education. Available through Comforty Media Concepts, 2145 Pioneer Road, Evanston, IL 60201. (708) 475-0791; fax: (708) 475-0793. This video focuses on two students who have been fully included in their local school program. It explores the encouraging effect such participation has had on their families' views of their futures.

Inclusion: Bernardsville Beginnings, VHS. Edited by In Focus, Bedminister, NJ. Available through National Down Syndrome Society, 666 Broadway, 8th Floor, New York, NY 10012. (800) 221-4602; fax: (212) 979-2873. A 23-minute video which follows Alison through her first full year in a first grade inclusion program. It is a step-by-step account of teaching staff preparation and classroom experience. The video presents a picture of one girl's successful adjustment to education in an inclusive environment and a whole class's maturation by the experience.

Sean's Story: Ready for School, VHS. Produced by ABC News. Available through ABC News Video Order Department. "Turning Point" segment from September 7, 1994. (800) 913-3434. This video portrays two different outlooks on the education of children with Down syndrome: inclusion versus a special school. It is a thoughtful portrayal of two families who choose different paths in an attempt to provide their children with the best education possible.

Together We're Better, VHS. Produced by Comforty Media Concepts. Available through Comforty Media Concepts, 2145 Pioneer Road, Evanston, IL 60201. (708) 475-0791; fax: (708) 475-0793. A series of three videos, which encourage inclusive approaches in school and community life. The videos feature Dr. Marsha Forest, Dr. Jack Pearpoint, and Ms. Judith Snow conducting a workshop on inclusion. They emphasize the necessity of adequate support systems and sustained, cooperative effort. The videos address the rewards and challenges of implementing an inclusive program.

Two Faces of Inclusion: The Concept and the Practice and Facing Inclusion Together through Collaboration and Co-Teaching, VHS. Produced by L. Burrello, J. Burrello, and J. Winninger. Available through CASE Research Committee, Indiana University-Smith Research Center, Suite 103A, 2805 E. 10th Street, Bloomington, IN 47405. (812) 855-5090. A two-video set addressing the multifaceted issue of inclusion. Interviews with Doug Biklen, Wayne Sailor, Tom Skrtic, and with administrators, teachers, and parents. The first video is narrated by Lou Brown, University of Wisconsin at Madison, and the second by Marilyn Friend, Indiana University.

With Kids My Age: Answers to Questions about Inclusion. Produced by Inclusion Works! Available through The ARC of Texas, 1600 West 38th, 200, Austin, TX 78731. (512) 454-6694. An honest look at inclusive education at the elementary and secondary school level. Students, parents, teachers, and school administrators address the most pressing questions about inclusion.

Videos: Disabilities

Aerobics Teacher. (11/04/99, Segment Two, T991104-02). ABC News Home Video, American Broadcasting Co., Inc.

An Introduction to: The Deaf Community. Sign Media, Inc., 4020 Blackburn Lane, Burtonsville, MD 20866.

Asperger Syndrome: Living Outside the Bell Curve. Peytral Publications, Inc., P.O. Box 1162, Minnetonka, MN 55345.

Autism Spectrum Disorders and the SCERTS Model: A Comprehensive Educational Approach. National Professional Resources, Inc., 25 South Regent Street, Port Chester, NY 10573.

The Challenging Kid—Assessment & Intervention. Peytral Publications, Inc., P.O. Box 1162, Minnetonka, MN 55345.

Collaboration for Inclusion Series. Excellent Enterprises, Inc., Lawrence, KS.

Differentiating Instruction. Association for Supervision and Curriculum Development, Alexandria, VA.

Enhancing Strategies Instructions: Critical Teaching Behaviors. Excellent Enterprises, Inc., Lawrence, KS.

F.A.T. City: How Difficult Can This Be? (A simulation of what it means to have a learning disability), Richard Lavoie, PBS Video, (800) 424-7963.

Helping Students Master Social Skills. Excellent Enterprises, Inc., Lawrence, KS.

Inclusion: Profiles of Successful Students. Association for Supervision and Curriculum Development, Alexandria, VA.

Inclusion: Strategies for the Classroom. Association for Supervision and Curriculum Development, Alexandria, VA.

Keys to Success in Learning Strategy Instruction. Excellent Enterprises, Inc., Lawrence, KS.

Learning Disabilities and Social Skills: Last One Picked...1st One Picked On. Richard Lavoie, PBS Video, (800) 424-7963.

Learning Disabilities–Learning Abilities: Children & Parents & School & Strengths. Vineyard Video Productions, P.O. Box 370, West Tisbury, MA 02575.

Learning Disabilities–Learning Abilities: The Teaching: What LD Students Need. Vineyard Video Productions, P.O. Box 370, West Tisbury, MA 02575.

Learning Disabilities–Learning Abilities: Understanding the Connection. Vineyard Video Productions, P.O. Box 370, West Tisbury, MA 02575

Snapshots 2: Mental Retardation, Behavior Disorders, Visual Impairment, Traumatic Brain Injury, Learning Disabilities, Behavior/Emotional Disorder. Allyn and Bacon, Boston.

The Special Child: Maximizing Limited Potential. Films for the Humanities and Sciences, Box 2053, Princeton, NJ 08543.

Standing Outside the Fire. Garth Brooks, The Video Collection, Volume 2. Nashville, TN: Capitol Records, 1996.

Successfully Educating Preschoolers with Special Needs. Edvantage Media, Inc., 12 Forrest Ave., Fair Haven, NJ 07704.

Teaching Religion to Students with Mental Retardation. Center for Ministry with People with Disabilities, University of Dayton, Dayton, OH 45469.

We're Not Stupid: Living with a Learning Difference. Media Projects, Inc., 5215 Homer Street, Dallas, TX 75206.

When the Chips Are Down...Strategies for Improving Children's Behavior. Richard Lavoie, PBS Video (800) 424-7963.

Books

ASCD. *Educating Everybody's Children: Diverse Teaching Strategies for Diverse Learners.* Alexandria, VA: Association for Supervision and Curriculum Development, 1995.

Armstrong, T. *In Their Own Way: Discovering and Encouraging Your Child's Personal Learning Style.* Los Angeles: Jeremy Tarcher, Inc., 1987.

Bener, W. N. *Differentiating Instruction for Students with Learning Disabilities.* Thousand Oaks, CA: Corwin Press, 2002.

Beninghof, A. M. *SensAble Strategies: Including Diverse Learners through Multisensory Strategies.* Longmont, CO: Sopris West, 1998.

Cole, S., B. Horvath, C. Chapman, C. Deschenes, D. Ebiling, and J. Sprague. *Adapting Curriculum and Instruction in Inclusive Classrooms: Staff Development Kit.* Bloomington, IN: Indiana Institute on Disability and Community, 1994.

DeBoer, A., and S. Fister. *Working Together: Tools for Collaborative Teaching.* Longmont, CO: Sopris West, 1996.

Divinyi, J. E. *Good Kids, Difficult Behavior: A Guide to What Works and Doesn't Work.* Peachtree City, GA: The Wellness Connection, 2000.

Dunn, K. B., and A. B. Dunn. *Trouble with School: A Family Story about Learning Disabilities.* Bethesda, MD: Woodbine House, Inc., 1993.

Dwyer, K. M. *What Do You Mean I Have a Learning Disability?* New York, NY: Walker and Company, 1991.

Gardner, H. *Frames of Mind.* New York, NY: Basic

Books, 1985.

Getskow, V., and D. Konczal. *Kids with Special Needs: Information and Activities to Promote Awareness and Understanding.* Huntington Beach, CA: The Learning Works, Inc., 1996.

Giangreco, M. F. *Quick Guides to Inclusion: Ideas for Educating Students with Disabilities.* Baltimore, MD: Brookes Publishing Co., 1997.

Grossman, H. *Classroom Behavior Management.* Oxford: Rowman & Littlefield, Publishers, 2004.

Hanson, M. J., and E. W. Lynch. *Understanding Families: Approaches to Diversity, Disability, and Risk.* Baltimore, MD: Paul H. Brookes, 2004.

Heacox, D. *Differentiating Instruction in the Regular Classroom: How to Reach and Teach All Learners, Grades 3—12.* Minneapolis, MN: Free Spirit Publishing, 2002.

Jackson, L., and M. V. Panyan. *Positive Behavioral Support in the Classroom: Principles and Practice.* Baltimore, MD: Paul H. Brookes, 2002.

Johnson, D. W., and R. T. Johnson. *Cooperation and Competition.* Edina, MN: Interaction Book Company, 1989.

Kameenui, E. J., and D. W. Carnine. *Effective Teaching Strategies that Accommodate Diverse Learners.* Columbus, OH: Prentice-Hall, 1998.

Katz, L., C. Sax, and D. Fisher. *Activities for a Diverse Classroom: Connecting Students.* Colorado Springs, CO: PEAK Parent Center, 1998.

Kaufman, S. Z. *Retarded Isn't Stupid, Mom!* Baltimore, MD: Paul Brookes Publishing, 1999.

Levine, D. A. *Building Classroom Communities: Strategies for Developing a Culture of Caring.* Bloomington, IN: National Educational Service, 2003.

Levison, L., and I. St. Onge. *Disability Awareness in the Classroom.* Springfield, IL: Charles C. Thomas, Publisher, 1999.

Maurice, C. *Behavioral Intervention for Young Children with Autism.* Austin, TX: Pro-Ed, 1996.

McConnel, K., G. Ryser, and J. Higgins. *Practical Ideas That Really Work for Students with ADHD.* Austin, TX: Pro-Ed, 2000.

McConnel, K., G. Ryser, and J. Higgins. *Practical Ideas That Really Work for Students with Dyslexia and Other Reading Disorders.* Austin, TX: Pro-Ed, 2003.

Miller, N. B., and C. C. Sammons. *Everybody's Different.* Baltimore, MD: Paul Brookes Publishing, 1999.

Murphy, D. A., C. C. Meyers, S. Olesen, K. McKean, and S. H. Custer. *Exceptions: A Handbook of Inclusion Activities for Teachers of Students at Grades 6–12 with Mild Disabilities.* Longmont, CO:

Sopris West, 1994

Pancsofar, E. *Positive Profiles: Building Community Together.* St. Augustine, FL: Training Resource Network, Inc., 1998.

Perske, R. *New Life in the Neighborhood: How Persons with Retardation or Other Disabilities Can Help Make a Good Community Better.* Nashville, TN: Abingdon Press, 1989.

Smith, T., E. Polloway, and J. Patton. *Teaching Students with Special Needs in Inclusive Settings.* Boston, MA: Allyn & Bacon, 2003.

Tileston, D. W. *What Every Teacher Should Know About Special Learners.* Thousand Oaks, CA: Corwin Press, 2004.

Vaughn, S., C. Bos, and J. Schumm. *Teaching Exceptional, Diverse, and At-Risk Students.* Boston, MA: Allyn & Bacon, 2003.

Wilkins, J. *Group Activities to Include Students with Special Needs.* Thousand Oaks, CA: Corwin Press, 2001.

Websites:

Agencies and Organizations

http://www.ideapractices.org/ (Information about special education law and recent developments in special education.)

http://www.teachnet.com (An excellent source for teaching ideas and resources.)

http://www.indiana.edu/cafs/ (The Center for Adolescent and Family Studies at Indiana University. Excellent resources and links to other helpful sites.)

http://www.resna.org/ (Technology for individuals with disabilities.)

http://www.dyslexia-add.org (Information on dyslexia, including materials and teaching ideas.)

http://oneaddplace.com (One of the best websites on teaching children with attention deficit disorders.)

http://www.dyslexiaonline.com

http://www.ldteens.org/

http://www.disabilityresources.org/

http://www.nichcy.org/ (National Information Center for Children and Youth with Disabilities. The place to go for information on characteristics and needs of children with disabilities.)

http://www.cec.sped.org/ (The Council for Exceptional Children)

http://www.ldanatl.org/ (Learning Disabilities Association)

http://www.add.org (National Attention Deficit Association)

http::/www.nfxf.org (National Fragile X Syndrome

Foundation)

http://www.aamr.org/ (American Association on Mental Retardation)

http://www.thearc.org (The ARC, formerly known as the Association for Retarded Citizens)

http://www.ndss.org (National Down Syndrome Society)

http://www.nofas.org (Fetal Alcohol Syndrome Organization)

http://www.reyessyndrome.org (National Reye's Syndrome Foundation)

http://www.sbaa.org (Spina Bifida Association of America)

http://www.tsa-usa.org/ (Tourette Syndrome Association)

http://www.ucpa.org/ (United Cerebral Palsy Association, Inc.)

http://www.williams-syndrome.org/ (Williams Syndrome Association)

http://www.pwsausa.org/ (Prader-Willi Syndrome Association)

http://www.autism-society.org (Autism Society of America)

http://www.acb.org (American Council of the Blind)

http:::www.nidd.nih.gov (National Institute on Deafness and Other Communication Disorders)

http://www.oraldeafed.org (Oral Deaf Education)

http://where.com/scott.net/asl (American Sign Language)

http://handspeak.com (Learning sign language)

http://cecp.air.org/index.htm (Center for Effective Collaboration and Practice)

http://www.hood.edu/seri/behavior.htm (SERI Behavior Disorder Resources)

http://www.biausa.org (Brain Injury Association)

http://www.efa.org (Epilepsy Foundation)

http://www.mdausa.org (Muscular Dystrophy Association)

http://www.cff.org (National Cystic Fibrosis Foundation)

http://www.asha.org (American Speech-Language-Hearing Association)

Parents and Families

http://www.kidsource.com/index.html (KidSource Online) KidSource Online provides parents and teachers with educational and health care information for children ranging from newborns through age eighteen. Tied to the Schwab Foundation for Learning (SFL), the information focuses mostly on learning "differences." It offers ideas for summer fun (books, videos, CDs one can order from their store), and articles for parents and teachers ranging from Learning Disabilities, to child safety, to classroom questions ("How do I ask questions that foster student achievement?") to summer camp information.

http://www.nppsis.org (National Parent to Parent Support and Information System, Inc.) This is a non-profit organization whose goal is to help families with children who have special health care needs and rare disorders. It offers a list of parent-to-parent programs throughout the U.S. and links to other national organizations.

http://www.ldonline.org (LD Online: The Interactive Guide to Learning Disabilities for Parents, Teachers, and Children) LD Online provides information to parents and teachers of learning-disabled students. It suggests motivational techniques for writing and includes personal testimonies which encourage other learning-disabled students to achieve their goals despite their disabilities.

http://www.circleofinclusion.org/ (Circle of Inclusion) The Circle of Inclusion site is designed for early childhood service providers and families of young children and provides demonstrations of information about the effective practices of inclusive educational programs for children from birth through age eight.

http://www.schwablearning.org/ (Schwab Foundation for Learning) The Schwab Foundation for Learning site is a hub of links which provide information, support, and hope for parents and educators helping kids with learning differences. There are links to research, publications, and resources for the parent and the teacher. This site is good for special education teachers, principals, and parents of children with disabilities.

http://www.ncld.org/ National Center for Learning Disabilities, Inc. (NCLD) The National Center for Learning Disabilities offers articles on recognizing disabilities, information on what a learning disability is, articles that explain the rights of LD children, and links to national organizations that support LD children and adults. It is designed for parents, teachers and anyone interested in learning disabilities.

http://www.npnd.org/ (The National Parent Network on Disabilities) The National Parent Network on Disabilities site provides organizational information, legislative updates, and access to services provided by the organization.

http://www.cdc.gov/ncbddd/adhd/ (Center for Disease Control) This site contains articles discussing the effects of ADHD on the individual's life. Also contains resources and links to other sites in regard to ADHD.

Bibliography

Affleck, M., Adams, and Lowenbraun. "Integrated Classroom versus Resource Model: Academic Viability and Effectiveness." *Exceptional Children* (1988): 339-348.

Armstrong, T. *The Multiple Intelligences of Reading and Writing*. Alexandria, VA: Association for Supervision and Curriculum Development, 2003.

Austin, S., and G. Meister. *Responding to Children at Risk: A Guide to Recent Reports*. Philadelphia, PA: Research for Better Schools, 1990.

Banerji, M., and R.A. Daily. "A Study of the Effects of an Inclusion Model on Students with Specific Learning Disabilities." *Journal of Learning Disabilities* 28 (1995): 511.

Barr, R.D., and W.H. Parrett. *Hope at Last for At-Risk Youth.* Boston, MA: Allyn & Bacon, 1995.

Berk, L., and A. Winsler. *Scaffolding Children's Learning: Vygotsky and Early Childhood Education*. Washington, DC: National Association for the Education of Young Children, 1995.

Bishop, M. "Inclusion: Balancing the Ups and Downs." *Momentum* 26, no.3 (1995): 28-30.

Collins, B.C., A. Epstein, T. Reiss, V. Lowe. "Including Children with Mental Retardation in the Religious Community." *Teaching Exceptional Children* 33, no. 5 (2001): 52-58.

Copple, C., ed. *A World of Difference: Readings on Teaching Young Children in a Diverse Society*. Washington, D.C.: National Association for the Education of Young Children, 2003.

Crockett, J.B. "Viable Alternatives for Students with Disabilities: Exploring the Origins and Interpretations of LRE." *Exceptionality* 8 no. 1 (2000): 43–60.

Crockett, J.B., and J.M. Kauffman. *The Least Restrictive Environment: Its Origins and Interpretations in Special Education*. Mahwah, NJ: Lawrence Erlbaum Associates, Inc., 1999.

Davis, S. *Report Card on Inclusion in the Education of Students with Mental Retardation*. Arlington, TX: The ARC, 1995.

Derman-Sparks, L. *The Anti-Bias Curriculum*. Washington, DC: National Association for the Education of Young Children, 1989.

Eckes, J. "The Power of Community," *The Power of Vision* 8 no.1(2003). The AbleNet Consortium for Excellence in Special Education.

Elias, M.J., H. Arnold, and C.S. Hussey, eds. *EQ+IQ=Best Leadership Practices for Caring and Successful Schools.* Thousand Oaks, CA: Corwin Press, 2003.

Flegal, D. *Sign & Say: Bible Verses for Children*. Nashville, TN: Abingdon Press, 1999.

Fuller, C., and L. Jones. *Extraordinary Kids: Nurturing and Championing Your Child with Special Needs.* Colorado Springs, CO: Focus on the Family, 1997.

Gardner, Howard. *Frames of Mind: The Theory of Multiple Intelligences.* New York, NY: Fontana Press, 1993.

Gartner, A. and D.K. Lipsky. "Beyond Special Education: Toward a Quality System for All Students." *Harvard Educational Review,* no. 57 (1987): 367-385.

Giangreco, M., and J. Putnam. "Supporting the Education of Students with Severe Disabilities in Regular Education Environments," in *Critical Issues in the Lives of People with Severe Disabilities,* edited by L.H. Meyer, C. Peck, and L. Brown, 245-70. Baltimore, MD: Paul H. Brookes, 1991.

Giensberg, A. "Spiritual Development and Young Children." *European Early Childhood Education Research Journal* 8 no. 2 (2000): 23-37.

Good, T., and J. Brophy. *Looking in Classrooms*. New York: Longman, 2000.

Gould, P., and J. Sullivan. *The Inclusive Early Childhood Classroom: Easy Ways to Adapt Learning Centers for All Children.* Saddle River, NJ: Merrill Prentice Hall, 1999.

Higgins, Judith, K. McConnell, J. Patton, and G. Ryser. *Practical Ideas That Really Work for Students with Dyslexia and Other Reading Disorders.* Austin, TX: PRO-ED, Inc., 2003

Johnson, D., R. Johnson, and E. Holubec. *Circles of Learning: Cooperation in the Classroom*. Edina, MN: Interaction Book Company, 1990.

Johnson, G.M. "Effectiveness of Interventions for At-Risk Students." *Special Services in the Schools*, no. 14 (1998): 77-103.

Jones, R., and D. Flegal. *More Sign & Say: Bible Verses for Children.* Nashville,TN: Abingdon Press, 2000.

Kaiser, B., and J.S. Rasminsky. *Challenging Behaviors in Young Children: Understanding, Preventing, and Responding Effectively.* Boston, MA: Allyn & Bacon, 2003.

Levine, D.A. *Building Classroom Communities: Strategies for Developing a Culture of Caring.* Bloomington, IN: National Educational Service, 2003.

Lavoie, R. *How Difficult Can this Be?,* Video. Washington, DC: Peter Rosen Productions/PBS/WETA, 1989.

McPartland, J.M., and R.E. Slavin. *Policy Perspectives: Increasing Achievement of At-Risk Students at Each Grade Level.* Washington D.C.: U.S. Department of Education, 1990.

Mercer, C.D., and A.R. Mercer. *Teaching Students with Learning Problems.* 6th ed. Columbus, OH: Merrill, 2001.

National Dissemination Center for Children with Disabilities. "Disability Fact Sheets." Washington, DC: October, 2003.

Roeser, R.W., J.S. Eccles, and A.J. Sameroff. "School as a Context of Early Adolescents' Academic and Social-Emotional Development: A Summary of Research Findings." *The Elementary School Journal,* no. 100 (2000): 443–71.

Ryser, Gail and Kathleen McConnell. *Practical Ideas That Really Work for Students with ADHD: Preschool through Grade 4.* Austin, TX: PRO-ED, Inc., 2005

School Linked Human Services: A Comprehensive Strategy for Aiding Students at Risk of School Failure. Washington, D.C.: U.S. General Accounting Office, 1993.

Smith, T.E., E.A. Polloway, J.R. Patton, and C.A. Dowdy. *Teaching Students with Special Needs in Inclusive Settings.* Boston, MA: Allyn and Bacon, 1998.

Strain, P., and M. Hemmeter. "Keys to Being Successful When Confronted with Challenging Behaviors." *Young Exceptional Children* 1, no. 1 (1997): 2-8.

Vygotsky, L.S. *The Collected Works of L.S. Vygotsky*, Vol. 2. Edited by R.W. Rieber & A.S. Carton. Translated by J.E. Knox & C.B. Stevens. New York, NY: Plenum, 1993.

Walker, H., and R. Sylwester. "Reducing Students' Refusal and Resistance." *Teaching Exceptional Children* 30, no. 6 (1998): 52-59.

Will, M. "Educating Children with Learning Problems: A Shared Responsibility." *Exceptional Children,* no. 52 (1986): 411-15.

Winning Ways: Creating Inclusive Schools, Classrooms, and Communities. Alexandria, VA: NASBE Publications, 1995.

York-Barr, J., T. Schultz, M.B. Doyle, R. Kronberg, and S. Crossett. "Inclusive Schooling in St. Cloud: Perspectives on the Process and People." *Remedial and Special Education* 17, no. 2 (1996): 92-105.

Bibliography

Index